Therapeutic Parenting

Its A Matter of Attitude!

Deborah Hage, MSW

For additional information or available books/videos
please contact:

Families by Design
PO Box 2812
Glenwood Springs, CO 81602

970 984-2222/ fax 970 876 0115
www.attachment.org

ISBN # O-9703525-7-3

Therapeutic Parenting
Its A Matter of Attitude!

Contents

To My Children:
     Rebecca
     Jonathan
     Matthew
     Ruben
     James
     Robert
     Rachel
     Jesse
     Amber
     Plus Brandon, Alex, Shari, and Verna
With gratitude for teaching me all I know.

To Connell Watkins and Nancy Thomas
     Who helped me make sense of what I was
     learning from my children!

And to Paul,
     Who stuck with me while I learned it!

Therapeutic Parenting
Its A Matter of Attitude!

David, A Love Story

David was adopted at six months of age. As the years passed it became evident to us, as well as a procession of therapists and psychologists, that while I took for granted David was my son, David felt very strongly I was not his mother. He appeared so angry at his birth mother for relinquishing him that any other mother figure was to be totally rejected. In his view, if even his birth mother could not be trusted to love him, how could I be trusted to love him?

The diagnosis for his particular emotional disturbance was "unattached" or "attachment disorder." What that meant in terms of day to day living was he neither wanted me as a mother nor trusted me to take care of him.

His nights were interrupted by terrorizing nightmares from which we could not waken him. His days were filled with trying to prove me incapable of being his mother and testing the extent of my love for him. If I said it was Monday, he disagreed. If I gave him potatoes, he wanted rice. If I said 2 plus 2 are 4, he said it was 5. If I said it was raining, he insisted it was snowing. If I praised his work, he tore it up. If I helped him build blocks, he kicked them down. If I hugged him close, he pushed me away. No matter how carefully I counted out peanuts or poured juice or dished out ice cream, he screamed that everyone always got more than he did.

And what did I do? I loved him. He was my son and his behavior towards me only served to convince me how much he needed to have proved to him he was loved and wanted, unequivocally, no strings attached. It was difficult, if not impossible at times, to not return the constant barrage of anger he hurled at me or to give in to his constantly changing demands.

My husband was enormously supportive through it all. Though, when he came home he saw a completely different child than I did during the day. At times he found it easier to believe there was nothing wrong with David, but a great deal wrong with me. Our other five children, three of which were also adopted, were doing so well I knew, despite the innuendos of others, it was not me, but David who was suffering the most. That knowledge of his *suffering forced me to continue loving him even after our pediatrician counseled us to relinquish him because he was too emotionally disturbed to live in a normal home and his behavior caused more tension than was healthy for a family to endure.*

I have loved David through running away, through public displays of uncontrollable anger, through countless times of being shoved aside, spat at, bit, hit, and punched. He has remained my son despite his need to sneak and hide food in his room until it rots and his inability or unwillingness to control where he puts his body wastes. Why? Because he is my son. He doesn't have to earn the privilege of being my son. He is not my son because he is a good boy. He is not my son because he loves me. He is my son, because he is my son.

The miracle is that love is winning. He started receiving holding therapy when he was eight and has since gone on Outward Bound, a two week wilderness experience. David is now 15 years old and time is showing me that my love is finally prevailing over the hurt he suffered over his birth mom's rejection. David talks to me, often nicely. He lets me help him. We tickle and touch, he even hugs me sometimes. Nothing dramatic, no overnight cures, just the second by second unrelentless love that I have for him is giving him a window on life as it can be.

Therapeutic Parenting

The therapeutic parents at the Attachment Center at Evergreen have written a handbook in which they define what they believe therapeutic parenting consists of. It states:

> *Therapeutic Treatment Parenting* is a professional approach to treating children and training parents of children with severe emotional disorders. The therapeutic parent is a highly skilled and trained individual who works in conjunction with a treatment team to treat the child in the therapeutic milieu of a family. The expertise and involvement of the treatment parent is the foundation of this unique approach. The treatment parent creates a therapeutic environment in which the team treatment plan is implemented on a 24 hour basis.... A treatment parent is committeed to children, committed to remaining emotionally stable and healthy, committed to remaining open to consideration of all therapeutic tools, committed to continuing education, and committed to a team approach.

The Attachment Center at Evergreen, Inc. <u>Parents of ACE Handbook</u>, 1995. The brochure for the Attachment Center at Evergreen further defines what is involved in parenting. It states:

Effective Parenting - Successful parenting involves high structure, effective environmental controls, helping the child develop appropriate responses to authority and the development of internal controls. Further it involves the use of logical and natural consequences, the reinforcement of reciprocity and nurturing/reparenting. Goals of parenting are: to prepare child for the real world and to help child learn to be respectful, responsible and fun to be around.

The Attachment Center at Evergreen, Inc. <u>Attachment Center Brochure,</u> 1995.

Communicating interventions appropriate for the parenting of emotionally and behaviorally problematic children is not so much to teach parents how to mold their children into responsible and cooperative human beings as it is to enable them to have the tools, desire and energy to stay their children's parents over the long haul. Going into any relationship with the aim of changing the other person into someone more easily loved has always been of dubious value. It is far more valuable to find ways to make the relationship work within the constraints of already developed personalities.

"The therapeutic parent realizes the abuse (emotional, sexual and physical) cannot be erased or forgotten, but the effects can be decreased" (<u>Parents of ACE Handbook</u>). This is the foundation of the techniques developed by therapeutic parents at The Attachment Center at Evergreen. Stopping a child from engaging in negative behavior is always nice, but many parents will be disappointed, discouraged and defeated if that is their primary goal.

So, the question is not, "How do we make our children more lovable?" Rather it is, "How do we love unlovable children?" Learning how to love children who have learned in the past that love hurts, who are afraid of love and who actively seek to rebuff love and the human contact it engenders is the essence of therapeutic parenting.

First Things First
Rule #1 : **Always take good care of yourself!**
Rule #2 : **Always take good care of yourself!**
Rule #3 : **When all else fails, make sure you take good care of yourself!**

Oddly enough, the first requirement of learning to love unlovable children is to love ourselves. What hope does a child have to learn how to love himself or others if the adults who are most present in his life don't demonstrate they love themselves? The message to the child is, "Look at the abuse and neglect you have suffered. Your experience has taught you that you are not entitled to being the recipient of loving concern when you are a child. By observing me and knowing I will let you abuse me you can tell that when you grow up you are not entitled to respect either."

Step one in therapeutic parenting is to take very good care of yourself and your significant relationships. It is important that parents take time out for themselves. Children need to see their negative behavior does not imprison their parents and prevent them from having a good time together. Parents need to demonstrate they are not going to be punished for their child's choices by allowing fear of the child's ability to misbehave be the focus of their lives. They need to actively seek, train and pay well for alternative care for their children several times a month for evenings out and at least once a year for extended vacations. This is not a luxury. It is essential for parents to be filled up by the one on one time involved in eye contact, touch, smiles, food, and movement before they can pass these essential ingredients of feeling loved on to their children. Children cannot receive from their parents qualities which their parents do not possess themselves.

Often parents are so much in love with their child they are willing to go to extreme lengths to help their child, to their own detriment. Parents attend workshops, read books, consult profressionals and listen to tapes in their zeal to be the exact kind of parent their child needs. They become adept at consequencing and applying numerous tools and interventions. This becomes counter-productive when parents believe they need to stick to a consequence because it will be a good opportunity for the child to learn at the expense of themselves. Parents should not apply a consequence that will hurt them. It is better to let the negative behavior slide or to take care of it later than it is to stick to an intervention that causes the parent to suffer in some way. If the family has tickets to a game and one child's behavior does not warrant his or her going, yet it is too late to find alternate care, go anyway. Consequence later. Don't allow resentment to build in the family or in the parents because everyone has been held hostage to one child's behavior, even if that means the poorly behaved child will get to do something or go somewhere he or she does not "deserve" to go.

When going out together is not a possibility then parents can take turns being "On Duty". This occurs when one parent has a higher level of energy than the other and takes over all child-parent interactions for an evening or a weekend. If a child should approach the mom who is quietly reading in her bedroom or recharging her batteries by soaking in a hot, scented tub, than the mom says, "Sorry, I'm off duty. You need to go talk to Dad about that."   Off duty hours can also be spent with those children in the family who are fun to be around. Oftentimes parents get so caught up in the drama of the "naughty child" they neglect the children who are loving and reciprocal. Leaving one parent in charge while the other rejoices in the fun of being with those children who often are left in the background due to the needs of the behaviorally problematic child is good for the entire family and models for everyone the rewards of cooperation and responsible actions.

Parents also need to have each other's disciplinary efforts validated in the presence of the child. Questioning the use of an intervention is often appropriate, however, it needs to be discussed in private. Parents who communicate to a disturbed child they are in disagreement about what to do increases that child's commitment to splitting and manipulation to the detriment of the marital relationship. The child will continue to use any behavior as long as he can get one parent to endorse it. Many therapeutic parents follow the dictum, "When parents are in disagreement the stricter parent decides."

A particularly effective way for father to support the beleaguered mother is to ask her when he returns home from work in the evening, "How were the kids for you today?" Those kids who did not wear her out get to continue playing. Those kids who were uncooperative are sent to their room, saying "Looks like you have drained Mom. I better spend some time with her to fill her back up." Dad spends one-on-one time with mother, listening to her day, helping her prepare dinner or giving her a back or foot massage. The message to the children is, "Mother is central to this family. If you are not going to make her life easier, then I will. I can't spend time with you when your mom needs me first."

What often happens, however, is the reverse. Dad comes home and finds Mom wiped out so offers to take the kids off her hands. The child who has so exhausted Mom she can't see straight, then gets rewarded by spending time with Dad while Mom is abandoned and left by herself. She is thinking, "The child was a jerk all day and now gets to have a fun time with Dad. He is so phony, saves up his enjoyable side for Dad, and Dad can't see it! When do I get fun times with either one of them?" While Dad is seeing the best side of the child, that has been hidden from Mom all day, he begins to think, "I wonder what is wrong with Mom that she can't get along with this child. He is certainly good for me." Dad needs to concentrate on Mom first. When she is being treated well by the children, then he can spend time with them. This will minimize triangulation in the family, consequence those children who are not cooperative and give Mom a boost.

When parents take good care of themselves and each other first and their children second, there is an optimum chance for everyone to enjoy life and living together.

A natural extension of parents who treat themselves and their children with a high degree of respect and loving care is having the children treat them that way as well. Let there be no mistake, however. Children do not need to treat their parents respectfully because parents need the boost to their egos. Children need to treat their parents with respect because that is how children learn self-respect.

Parents, teachers, and other adults who tolerate disrespect are saying to children, "I am not worthy of respect." The children then say to themselves, "If I can treat others with disrespect and get away with it then people can treat me with disrespect and get away with it. None of us are worth anything at all, not even me." The damage done to a child's self-esteem when he or she is allowed to whine, curse, swear and, in numerous other forms of speech and behavior, be disrespectful of the loving authorities in their life is incalculable.

How do parents manage this two faceted task of care-giving and care-taking? The answer lies in therapeutic parenting. Therapeutic parenting is implementing those techniques which encourage us to take care of ourselves and our children and which put in place the reciprocal nature of being truly loving so children respond by taking good care of themselves and of their relationship with us. It is not taking the power to change children too seriously, but taking the power to love in constructive ways very seriously.

Pro-active and Re-Active Approaches

Being a therapeutic parent is approached from two directions simultaneously - *pro-active* and *re-active*.

Being *proactive* means setting up a home and environment which is fun for children to be in. Creating a place for children that is warm, welcoming, respectful and fun encourages the children to practice behaviors which allow them to stay there. Being a parent who is 'in tune" with the child, sensitive to the non-verbal messages of behavior enables a child to see he is loved even when his behavior is unlovable. If home is not a safe haven for children it will seem pointless for them to change their behavior in order to live there. In fact the opposite may occur. Children who do not perceive they are in a caring environment could deliberately choose negative behaviors which will cause them to be moved. Consciously designing an inviting family setting is pivotal to both the well being of the child and the well being of the parents.

Being pro-active also means identifying and taking advantage of the necessary tools and resources to heal the child. Just as parents need to be sensitive to the child, the child needs to become sensitive to the world, aware of and caring about how his behavior affects others. Researching medications, brain development, nutrition and therapeutic interventions and how they can be utilized to contribute to the child and family's well being is important.

Setting family tone, however, is not enough. *Re-active* parenting techniques ensure when negative behavior does occur it is met with firm kindness and respect while placing the child in the position of having to take responsibility for his or her behavior.

During both proactive and reactive parenting therapeutic parents make sure they demonstrate to the children they take good care of themselves first. When they choose to participate in something fun for the child they make sure it is fun for them also. Likewise, when a child's negative behavior requires a response, the parents ensure that regardless of how the child reacts to the consequence of his behavior, the parents feel good about themselves and the child so they are able to continue to care for the child. When parents are firm about what they are going to do, not what they are going to make their child do, win-win situations are created and ego-crunching defeat is avoided for everyone.

The <u>pro-active approach</u> is used to avoid problems and encourage positive behavior. The <u>re-active approach</u> is used as a response to negative behavior.

Both work simultaneously and involve touch, eye contact, food and smiles. In neither is communication done principally with words. Both approaches are based on actions.

Pro-active Therapeutic Parenting
<u>Critical Elements Necessary for Attachment to Occur</u>

People do not just "fall in love". Watch adolescents in a high school and it will be clear what a teen does in order for another teen to take notice. Their dance is universal to the mating dances of the world. The first thing a young boy does is watch the object of his affections to see if she looks back. Accompanying this glance is a smile, tentative at first, then more steady. When she looks back and smiles as well, both know contact has been made. Words are exchanged. What they are is irrelevant. The next step is to establish physical contact. They "bump into" or brush up against either other. If neither flinches away another level of contact has been established. As tentative touches, eye contact, conversation and smiles progress to a more steady, equally acceptable level, food is incorporated. First formal dates usually involve sharing food. Food gifts follow, consisting of chocolate or other sweet – never carrots or broccoli! Typically subsequent dates will involve car rides, amusement parks, walking, bike riding, roller skating – anything that involves movement. Ultimately, preferably after marriage, but all too frequently before, the growing intimacy results in sexual activity, which incorporates all of the elements – eye contact, reciprocal smiles, vocalizations, touch and movement, with food usually integrated immediately before or after.

These elements are cornerstone to any intimate relationship whether it is between courting adolescents, married partners, or parents and children. Try to imagine being involved in a relationship where partners do not look at each other, smile at each other, talk with each other, touch each other, eat with each other, or do things together? It would be empty of meaning. When one partner seeks more of these elements than the other wants to provide resentment occurs. The parent and child relationship is no different. These elements must be present in order for parent and child to "fall in love" with each other.

When a baby is born the elements are incorporated naturally. The infant cries, expressing a need. Because the infant's ability to communicate is limited to vocalizations the crying, cooing, screaming and coughing must be interpreted by an adult who is in tune with what the child is trying to express. The adult, usually the mother, comes quickly to meet the infant's needs by <u>doing something</u> in response. The mother does not just say to the child, "I love you", and expect the child's needs to be met. The mother vocalizes, smiles, touches, feeds, moves and looks at her child. All of these actions combined cause chemicals in the brain of the child to release and flood the child with a sense of relaxation. The infant learns his needs are important to another person and they will be taken care of. He learns he is so important that when he expresses a need someone will come and he will feel better. He learns to trust the universe is a friendly, welcoming place and his happiness matters. He learns he can continue to ask for what he needs and wants, with the expectation he will be satisfied. He learns that to be in the presence of someone who cares for him enough to meets his needs and be there when he calls makes him feel very good and floods him with a sense of well being. That flooding sensation is the result of a chemical release and we call it "love". The psychotherapeutic world calls it "bonding" or "attachment."

<u>Bonding and Attachment are Functions of the Brain</u>
People like to believe "falling in love" is an emotional state. It is. However, it is also a physical state caused by chemicals in the brain being released in response to pleasure. The brain then becomes "wired" to reinforce the behaviors which produced the pleasurable circumstances, thus setting the stage for the behaviors to be repeated and the circumstances to occur again. This "wiring" takes place in utero and during the first two years of life. Since the majority of brain growth and learning takes place in the early years, once the brain's patterns are set they are very difficult to change. Not impossible, but difficult. The infant is "father to the man". If a child learns his cries will not be answered and his needs will not be met he learns the world is not a safe place to be and no one cares about him. If a child is abused he learns the world is painful. Either way his brain is wired for self-preservation, not attachment. He may be removed from the early abusive and neglectful environment and may, if he is lucky, get wonderful nurturing parents. While the external environment is radically different, the internal environment, dictated to the child by the patterns set in his brain, continues on the same path.

A child's brain creates his world. It is not a matter of reality as others see it but the perception of reality as the child sees it, that determines behavior!

Society is used to thinking of attachment disorders as being primarily indicated by negative behaviors. The negative behaviors are not the starting point, however. Preceding the destructive, withdrawn behaviors is brain damage caused by abuse and neglect in the first years of life. **Abuse and neglect in the first years of life cause brain damage. It is the brain damage which causes the negative behaviors and which keep the behaviors in place long after they have reason to be still occurring.**

Therapeutic parenting therefore, has numerous facets. Creating a home environment in which the brain can heal is one aspect. Nutrition and medication also effect brain growth and development and must be utilized. Lastly, therapeutic parenting interventions and developmental play can have a profound effect and help the brain rewire itself and repair the damage. All aspects are critical in helping children develop a capacity for new skills and behaviors.

Therapeutic Parenting Techniques Which Reinforce and Accentuate Bonding

(This series of interactions has been developed and put into place in thousands of families by Connell Watkins. They are useful as a means of giving parents a step by step guide to increase the affectional ties between them and their children. As in any of the thoughts and interventions suggested parents can do them completely right and still not get the desired results. Conversely they can do them all wrong or leave them out and the children still turn out fine. Parenting is an art, not a science. Sometimes A + B = C and sometimes X + R = C. Sometimes, C cannot be achieved regardless of what parents do. Despite our best hopes, wishes and dreams children are not programmable robots.)

1   *Any demonstration of affection on the parent's terms, not the child's, will accentuate bonding even if, and in spite of, the child's lack of responsiveness.*

Many children who have been abused and neglected are resistant to touch and affection. They are not used to it. It does not feel good. In fact, it is scary and arouses feelings of anger and fear, not love and connectedness. In their past touch became associated with pain, physical abuse or sexual abuse. Their memory banks store myriad examples of when parents touched them and they were hurt. It is easy to understand that their defenses against touch, such as pulling away, developed in response to pain and, for them, are completely natural and rational.

That said, refusing to allow touch is not acceptable and the defense mechanisms which were so useful when they were in an abusive situation no longer serves the child well. Once a child is in a safe, nurturing home with loving parents he needs to learn a whole new set of behaviors, more in keeping with the expectations of the world. To not teach a child who has been abused to accept and give touch is to teach him he is unlovable and dooms him to future relationships which are just as unhealthy as the ones he left behind. He will have difficulty relating to either his spouse or his children in meaningful, healthy ways. In other words, simply because a behavior is understandable does not mean it is acceptable.

Breaking down the walls of resistance to touch can be likened to taming a wild animal. It needs to be done softly, gently, and persistently. One technique is called the "touch and run". As the parent walks past the child she tousles the child's hair, gives him a quick hug, or light tickle. She needs to be in and out of the child's space before the child has time to flinch away or react negatively. Brushing a child's hair, doing a daughter's nails, and helping a child dress, are all ways of achieving contact in non-threatening ways. Blowing kisses brings a smile to the child's face even though no phsyical touch was involved. It is also useful to occasionally just grab the child in a big bear hug. If the child stiffens the parent can say in a loving way, "When you are so stiff like that or pull away from me I know its because you haven't received enough hugs in your young life. It is lucky for you that I am great at hugging and can fill you up.

Sweet food lovingly given is another cornerstone of bonding and attachment. Many of the techniques which are suggested are used in the company of candy. Children who are empty or who are accustomed to parenting themselves because they have learned through early experiences no one else can be trusted, need to see their parents as the source of goodness and light. Connecting candy to the parents is superficial – yet for many children it is the only opening available. Parents need to make the holes in their child's heart more important than the holes in their teeth. To that end , many therapeutic parents provide their children with fanny packs filled with candy. Everytime their child eats one during the day he makes a subliminal connection to his parents. Sugar spells love. No one sends porkchops on Valentine's Day! Caramels are particularly effective as, in addition to the sweet melting in the mouth, there is great movement of the jaws which causes labyrinthine stimulation. The stimulation of the hairs in the inner ear cause a chemical to release which floods the child with well being. Connecting that sense of well-being to the parents is an important component of bonding.

We adopted a child who had been severely abused and bed times were not occasions for snuggles and cuddles but aroused great fear. My son would cower against the wall, as far from the edge of the bed as he could get. Hugging him good night was the last thing that eased him into sleep. For several months I would sit on the edge of his bed and stroke his pillow as I talked quietly to him through it. When I had completed our evening prayers I would kiss his pillow and tell him he could not help but receive my love as he would get my kiss as soon as he put his head on the pillow. Gradually he moved his head closer and closer to the pillow and then we began a different game. I would playfully put the kiss on the tip of my finger and then find a place to touch him lightly. Over the weeks I would bend ever closer to him until the space between my lips and his face was smaller and smaller and my finger had to progress through an increasingly smaller distance. It took 6 months before I could land a kiss on his forehead without his flinching.

2. Any activity between parent and child that is on the parents' terms and involves eye contact, touch, movement, food, smiles and laughter.

Critical to successfully integrating this into the parenting repertoire of tricks is that it must be <u>on the parents' terms</u>. When two people have a relationship and one always initiates the loving interactions and words while the other responds, the one consistently doing the initiating gradually begins to feel decidedly unloved. Questions arise, "If I am loved why doesn't my spouse ever think to tell me so first? Why do I never get loving words or affectionate touch except in response to mine?" Children are no different. Parents can respond when their child initiates bonding actions, but they are not as meaningful to the child. They do not have the same bonding impact as when the parent initiates and the child responds. Actually, for some children, initiating the affection is a way for them to take control and make sure they get what they want on their terms, not on anyone else's. When a child is in control then bonding is not occurring.

Consciously taking control of a specific amount of play time each day is a key therapeutic concept presented in Vi Brody's excellent book <u>Developmental Play Therapy</u> and Anne Jernberg's equally important book <u>Theraplay</u>. <u>Messy Activities and More</u> by Virginia Morin was not written from a therapeutic perspective but is nonetheless very creative in the games it proposes. All deserve space on the shelves of both parents and therapists who find themselves dealing with children who are resistant to interacting with their parents and peers. Of the hundreds of games which can be used for bonding and attachment purposes only a few will be shared here. These must incorporate a sense of fun and laughter, otherwise the bonding usefulness is lost.

Wheel barrow
Trust walks – The child is blindfolded and the parents leads him around the room and over
    obstacles.
This Little Piggy – Use both toes and fingers.
Walking cheek to cheek.
Create a special handshake
Hug tag, Kiss tag

Blowing Bubbles – The child sits crosslegged, quietly on the floor, back straight, hands in lap and stays that way until Mom says "Go". When child is sitting appropriately Mom blows bubbles and says, "Go". Child jumps up and stomps and claps out bubbles. When all are popped the child must assume the strong sitting position in order for Mom to blow more bubbles.

Tower of hands

Catch

Cotton ball blow – A cotton ball is placed on the floor between the parent and child, who are laying on the floor facing each other and holding hands. The object is to blow the ball back and forth between them.

Patty-cake - Can also be done with feet

Mother May I

Water fight with squirt guns

Pillow Walk – Put pillows on the floor and space them so participants can jump and hop from one to the other across the room.

Lotion – Ask child to show where he has hurts, scratches, or bruises on his body which need attention. Gently rub lotion on each spot, perhaps adding a quick kiss to the "owie". This is an excellent bed time activity. (It is often believed when children are too easily hurt the best way to diminish the child's hypersensitivity to pain is by ignoring it. Actually the reverse is true. By initially paying attention to the bumps and scrapes of childhood the child's resistance to pain is raised, not lessened.)

Feather tickle – Gently tickle child with feather somewhere while his eyes are closed. Have him guess where you touched him with the feather.

Letter Writing – Draw a letter on the child's back with your finger and see if he can identify which one it is.

Massage – Massage child's feet/back/neck/hands etc. Child reciprocates, not necessarily at the same time. Suggested other times would be before Mom begins making dinner, when mom does child's laundry, when Dad fixes a bike, and other times when it would be appropriate for the child to give back or show gratitude for something a parent has done. If it is not convenient to get a massage at the time, parent can collect an IOU to be paid back during story time in the evening. A wonderful oil like lavender would have an added benefit.

Brush, comb child's hair

Feeding child – Feed candy, raisins, favorite foods. Make sure eye contact is reciprocal before putting the food in the child's mouth.

Rock A-bye Baby

Face paints, nail polish

Nose rub – This is a fun way to "kiss" with kids who are hug and kiss resistant.

Two Parent Games

>Two parent swing – The child lays down in a blanket which the parents pick up and swing between them.

>Back and forth – The child hops, runs, rolls, somersaults, walks backward between the adults who happily call, greet and encourage him. They can grab him up in a big hug, swing child around and then send him back to other adult.

>Hiding and Finding – One parent hides with child while other parent looks. They can hide under a blanket and then joyfully erupt from under blanket when found.

My daughter, adopted at age 4, was very resistant to eye contact. We would play peek-a-boo with M&Ms. I told her we would both cover our eyes. When I said "peek-a-boo" she was to open her eyes, look into mine and I would pop an M&M in her mouth. She would continue to get M&Ms as long as her eyes were locked on mine. After several weeks she was able to hold my gaze indefinitely. I then changed the rules. She would get an M&M everytime she came when I called and looked into my eyes. This one took much longer to master, however gradually, in response to my calling her name, she was able to call out reciprocally, "Yes, Mom" and come running for the M&Ms which would I would laughingly, with high praise, pop into her mouth. Note I did not give them to her to feed herself. From my hand to her mouth, from my heart to hers.

3. Parenting interactions which encourage the child responding according to the parents biorythms.

A basic skill of a bonded child is to be able to follow the parents' lead. Part of incorporating a parent's values is incorporating the way a parent does numerous small activities throughout the day. Parents need to be in tune with their child's needs, by watching for body posture, voice inflection. activity level, etc. By observing their child they learn much about the child's emotional and physical state at the time. By the same token, children need to learn to read their parents' facial expressions, posture, non-verbal gestures and voice inflections in order to learn more about the relationship and the interaction then is being overtly stated. When they can do this with their parents it can be generalized to their peer population, teachers and employers. Non-verbal cues to a person's state of mind is important to socialization. Being in tune and able to read the subtle nuances of the body language of others is an important part of what it means to be "attached", both to one's parents and to society as a whole. The following playful exercises help children practice following a parent's lead and being "in sync" with others.

Marching – Parent marches in different fashions. Big steps, short steps, high steps, shuffles, running, skipping, very slow, forward, backward, etc. The goal is for the child to match the parent as she marches through the room, around the furniture, up and down the stairs, in and out of doors, etc. The parent and child can take turns leading, however, as said before, the important bonding piece occurs when the parent leads.

This exercise does not need to be done all at the same time. When dinner is called Mom can say, "Time to hop to the table." "Walk backward to the table." In the evening, Dad can march the kids around the room in some fashion before playing "Ring Around The Rosy" and everyone falling down where they will sit to listen to the bedtime story.

Whistle Blow – This game is similar to marching except everyone has a whistle. The whistle can then be blown loud, soft, quickly, slowly, to a specific beat, etc.

Voice modulation – This game is also similar to marching except the voice is used. Parents can use loud, soft, a specific note, a specific beat, a specific sound, etc

Kicking, clapping – Similar to above only hands and feet are used.

Singing together – Old MacDonald, Twinkle Twinkle Little Star, etc.

Reciting nursery rhymes

Finger plays

Rocking

Toy Talk – The parent and child each take a figure toy and have them talk to each other. Make up a story which the two toys act out together.

Read outloud to child – This is an activity which would be very beneficial to have "ritualized". Every night at the same time read a similar number of stories and end with the same story book. Value Tales (ex. The Value of Honesty – a Biography of Abraham Lincoln), religious stories, stories with moral lessons, biographies, and histories, can all be used as it is a great time to communicate to the child the parent's values. Make sure the illustrations and stories are exciting to the child and not merely "preachy", otherwise you will end up communicating the subliminal message that your values are boring. The ending book would preferably be of a very simple rhythmic nature which the child would begin to memorize and say along. Good Night Moon, Runaway Bunny, I'll Love You Forever, and others like them are excellent. (Jabberwocky, illustrated by Graeme Baese was my children's favorite.) Chapter books can be used when the children are older. Indian in the Cupboard, Chronicles of Narnia, James and the Giant Peach and The Phantom Tollbooth easily hold a child's attention, even though they have few pictures. Remember, reading out loud must be done with animation and excitement.

4. Joint tasks where the child and parent are working together in a reciprocal way.
Working with a child must initially incorporate fun and enjoyment. Communicating to the child that work is hard, unenjoyable and anger producing is counter productive to the long term goal of helping a child become self-sufficient. Tasks must be made fun and/or even ridiculous. Once accomplished, a game or sweet must always be the reward. Working for free is a higher skill which not even all adults have mastered. Most of the time adults get paid for their work and children must see the rewards are worth the effort. Additionally if the reward is to be associated with the completion of a task, it must be given as quickly as possible as many children do not have a high sense of delayed gratification. It does not need to be big and if it is to be used for bonding, the reward must somehow be tied into doing something fun with mom or dad. Purchasing a toy or going out for a meal as a reward is counterproductive to bonding. If it is a small task then popping an M&M into the child's mouth is sufficient. The point is to connect work with sweetness and goodness.

Putting away groceries
Cleaning
Cooking (<u>Kids in the Kitchen</u> is a good initial cookbook for parents and children)
Making bed
Folding clothes
Washing dishes
Setting table

Remember: Parent laughing + child laughing = bonding

5. Any activity, no matter how small, that the child completes on the parent's terms enables the child to feel he or she is able to give back.
Children do not acquiesce to a parent's request for help because the parent is incapable of doing something for herself or because she is "She who must be obeyed." They must learn complete tasks for parents because it is good for them and helps make them less ego-centric and more reciprocal. They learn:
- they can contribute to the well being of another person or group of people
- maintaining a home and family is an enormous job and takes cooperative effort
- they can feel good about helping and
- it is appreciated.

Children who grow up understanding the work involved in growing and maintaining relationships and homes are less apt to jump into the decision to do so lightly as they approach adulthood.

Requests, are simply that, requests. They are not demands so must begin with "Please" and end with "Thank you." If the child refuses, then the parent can either do it for herself or forget about it. Failure to do these activities is not consequenced as this is not about taking or maintaining control. This is about giving children numerous opportunities to be reciprocal. When starting, the smaller the request the better. The request must be so small it is not even a blip on the child's defensive radar.

When the parent's arms are full, "Please grab my purse as you come in from the car."
While cooking, "Please get me an onion from the refrigerator."
When going out, "Please close the door behind us."
"If you're going through the kitchen could you please bring me a banana?"
"On your way out could you please put the mail in the mail box?"
"I forgot to put the napkins on the table. Could you please get them?"

6. Active listening to the child's behavior, keeping in mind children act out what they cannot verbalize.

For the most part the abuse and neglect children experienced occurred before they were able to talk. Since the emotional damage was preverbal then the ways they express their emotional barometer is non verbal as well. Children who were scared as infants, act scary and take such enormous risks with their behavior they are often described as self-destructive. Children who were abandoned as infants, isolate themselves and behave in such a way they push people away. Children who raged as infants with no one coming to take care of them, act out in anti-social, destructive and angry ways. Children who were sexually abused, masturbate and act out in sexual ways. They also tend to have poor hygiene in order to make sure no one wants to touch them. Children who distance themselves and whose eyes glaze over when they are disciplined were often so severely abused they emotionally leave when confronted. They no longer look as if they are present because in the past when they were abused they had to dissociate themselves from the pain in order to keep a part of them alive. In short, be sensitive when looking at the behavior and it is often diagnostic of what happened to them.

There is a reason why they are behaving the way they are behaving. At one point in time it was an effective self-defense mechanism and helped them stay alive. The problem is the behaviors which enabled them to survive are now counter-productive to creating a happy life and healthy relationship with those who are now learning to love them. They are now safe and no longer being hurt but their behavioral patterns have not changed to fit their new situation.

It is not that children are happy or feel self-fulfilled when their behaviors are distancing and destructive. Whatever level of pleasure they exhibit from their negative behaviors is due to their sense of accomplishment that they have been successful in keeping others at bay. They feel secure in their knowledge that once again they have been able to hurt before they were hurt or have been able to protect themselves from being hurt again.

Several techniques help children get past the pain in their history to accept the love in their present.

Normalize feelings. Children feel badly enough about themselves and their behaviors without living with the impression they are abnormal or possessed by the devil, views which are commonly held by children with severe negative behaviors. Several phrases help a child understand themselves better and see that, in their own way, due to their own personal history, they are behaving in very rational, understandable ways. The problem is those behaviors no longer work for them and are, in fact, counterproductive to their ultimate happiness.

"It is no wonder you broke your toys. When you were a baby someone broke your heart. I hope some day your heart will allow you to take care of precious things."

"Someone must have hurt you very badly that you feel you need to talk to me like that. It doesn't feel good to me so I know it didn't feel good to you."

"Boy, you sure are stiff when I hug you. I bet when you were a baby, love hurt."

"In this family we don't touch each other like that, but I bet in other places where you have lived that is how people showed they cared about each other. We show we love each other in different ways. Once you learn them you will enjoy living here more."

Child imitates pace and inflections of parent's voice - Parent finds a simple word or phrase and then says it in a variety of ways, with the child copying the parent's intonations. For example, say, "Please pass the peas" in an angry way, sarcastically, lovingly, softly, laughingly, demanding, whining, eagerly, and fearfully. This will enable children to hear the nonverbal message behind their words and the emotions and feelings they are communicating each time they speak.

Encourage the appropriate expression of feelings, show acceptance, and explore choices child has made in handling feelings, Help the child see and understand related consequences of different choices.

One of our sons had a very destructive streak of anger which would erupt at unpredictable times. When it did we would send him out to the back yard with a hammer and nails and tell him to pound them into the fence until he felt better. When he was in a good mood he would go pull them out.

7. Model handling strong feelings well.

Part of normalizing a child's internal feelings of fear, anger and grief is to accept them in ourselves. When parents deny they have strong feelings or cover them up the subliminal message to the child is that feelings are inappropriate and when you grow up you no longer have them. That is obviously not the message we want to communicate. What parents need to communicate is not that strong feelings are to be denied, but they are to be handled in appropriate ways. It is OK to be angry. It is not OK to hurt someone.

When many of the children we live with were growing up they learned anger meant pain. When a parent became angry they became out of control, things were broken, and people were hurt. In the current home children need to see people still get angry, but when they do it is handled differently. To deny strong feelings exist is to create a standard which the child knows he can never live up to. He knows he gets extremely angry and if adults never get angry then he is lost. Parents need to model getting angry and handling it well. They need to get angry and demonstrate how they conquer it. Parents can go to their room, go for a walk, eat something sweet, talk it over, or whatever they choose. The point is to demonstrate to their child that anger is a normal reaction to many of life's events and it can be controlled and managed in appropriate ways.

8. Promote feeling of continuity with child's past.

Children are a composite of their genetics and their experiences. Obviously, critical to their genetics is their biological parents. For most children with negative behaviors, their early life experiences are also intricately interwoven with their birth parents. The child is a part of his parents and a living, breathing representation of them.. To reject the people who gave the child his appearance, intelligence, and many of his mannerisms is to reject the child. Making a child aware of, and grateful for the positive gifts which he received from his parents is part of making a child comfortable with and accepting of himself.

Body Awareness – Any exercises and games which call attention to the intricacy and
   wonder of a child's body and its numerous abilities can be used to make a positive
   connection to the birth parents and their wondrous contributions to the child's life –
   even to the gift of life itself.
Mirror work – Stand the child in front of a mirror and have him point out his nose.

Exclaim what a wonderful nose he has and that his particular nose was a gift from his parents. It does its job exactly the way it was designed and fits his body perfectly. Go through the rest of his body, admiring each finger, toe, strand of hair, eye, tooth, ear, and freckle. This does not need to be done all at one time, but a different body part can be referred to every time the child brushes his teeth or combs his hair.

Listen to Heart Beat – Take the child's pulse or put your ear to his chest and listen to his heart. Exclaim how strong it is and what a wonderful gift of life it represents from his birth parents.

What Will Happen When I Push This Button? - Touch different body parts and ask child what noise it makes when it is touched. For example, the nose could squeak, the ears honk, the hair neigh, etc. This needs to be played with a great deal of laughter.

Wiggle one finger/arm/let/foot/nose, etc. at a time

Create a life book – Pictures and stories from the child's past need to be gathered Together. The child needs to see he has a distant past (which he doesn't remember), a past (which he may remember only slightly), a recent past (which he can remember clearly), a present, and future. His past and his future are filled with people who care. There are whole books on how to help a child create a life book, so no details will be provided here. Know, however, that life books are extremely important for children to see they did not just drop down from Mars and they are the way they are and who they are because of what has happened to them in the past.

In creating the life book make sure contact ismade with significant others from the child's past where appropriate. Collect stories and pictures from foster parents, birth family, teachers, childhood friends, neighbors, etc. Find ways to frame previous significant others in a positive light. Be advised if a parent rejects anyone significant to the child the child will internalize the rejection and reject the rejecting parent.

Pitcher Ceremony - Gather enough glasses so each one can represent a significant person in the child's past and present life. Get a large pitcher. Fill the glasses with water. Pour the first glass into the pitcher and tell the child the pitcher represents him and the glass of water represents all the good gifts he received from his birth mother as well as the negative experiences. Among other things like appearance, intelligence, gifts, etc, her contribution to his life was his life. Pour in the second glass and explain it represents his birth father. Talk about his contributions to who he is now. Each subsequent glass is another significant other (teachers, caseworkers, foster parents, birth relatives, etc.) Explain each person's contribution to who he is. Last, pour in the glass of water which represents his parents now. Talk about their gifts to him. Tell him to look at the pitcher and see if he can tell which drops of water came from his birthmother or birthfather. Which drops came from the other people he has come in contact with? He can't? That is because they are all a part of him and each has made a unique contribution to who he is right now. It is up to him to use all that he has to create his own future.

Some of a child's mannerisms which a parent might find annoying might not be a reflection of the child's desire to annoy but part of the child's genetic endowment. It is important to separate genetic behaviors out and not get too preoccupied with changing them.

Our son ate slightly hunched over his plate, shoveling food in from the back of his plate into his mouth. We consequenced the poor eating posture and habits continually until we had an opportunity to eat with members of his birth family - who all ate hunched over their plate, shoveling food in from the back into their mouths!

9. Redo early developmental stages the child has missed in fun, loving ways on the parent's terms, on a regular basis.

Many children did not participate in the normal parent-child interactions others take for granted. No one sang to the child, rocked the child, slept with the child or played peek-a-boo with the child. No one was there to put together puzzles or play board games. These activities are not just parental fluff, which the child can either experience or not and still grow up the same. Children need these activities in order to promote brain, physical and emotional growth. Without them the brain does not get wired along the pathways which are the most useful for future development. In other words, they are essential! The book Ghosts From the Nursery by Robin Karr-Morse and Meredith Wiley goes into detail regarding what happens to young brains when children do not get their developmental play needs met. Children who did not participate in these activities, still need them. They need to be filled up and nurtured much like a young infant. Rocking a child, singing lullabyes, putting puzzles together, and feeding with a bottle or box drink are all good ways to redo the missed developmental play. If children are older many of the games a child would have played as an infant but didn't can be redone while babysitting. When parent and child babysit for another even smaller child, the three of them can play the games which the child missed with the toddler without the child being made to feel infantile.

Eye Contact, Smiles, Touch, Nurturing, Developmental Play Take Time

Each of the above exercises and games takes time. There are no short-cuts. With a child who is emotionally needy quantity time and quality time cannot be differentiated. It requires a quantity of quality time to have an impact. A great deal of time spent one-on-one with each child is important to the development of a parent-child relationship. Twenty minutes a day of one on one time, during which the parent plays with the child and interacts with the child is minimal. Positive behaviors must be noted. Negative behaviors minimized. Time spent listening must outweigh time spent talking.

Therapeutic parents act on the belief there must be at least five positive interactions with a child for every negative interaction for bonding to occur. Sometimes children get into their issues so quickly after getting up in the morning it is advantageous for the parent to enter the bedroom and give 5 positives to the child before his feet even hit the floor. It can also be helpful to keep track of the time it takes after a bonding contact involving eye contact, touch, movement or food for the child to misbehave. Knowing how long a child can maintain good behavior allows the parent to intentionally interact with the child in a bonding way in the minutes, or seconds, prior to when an incident could be reasonably expected to occur.

Game playing, cuddling, rocking, and occasionally feeding a bottle to an unattached child is part of the life of the therapeutic parent. Specific methods for holding and snuggling with a child are dealt with in the book Holding Time by Martha Welch. The author goes into great detail on one technique, which, when used in concert with others, is helpful in creating a close, nurturing relationship.

Time spent cooking for or with a child is never wasted. Filling a home with the good smells of home-cooked meals is one of the best gifts a parent can give a child. "Nothin says lovin like somethin from the oven" is an old advertising jingle which captures the essence of this principle.

Time is a critical factor when it comes to volunteer activities as well. It is no accident. The same people who make the best parents for their own children also make excellent volunteers in the lives of other people's children. Being a den leader, Sunday School teacher, classroom aide, soccer coach, etc, are all admirable, worthy endeavors. Parents must guard, however, they do not get so involved in working with other children they neglect their own. Activities must be prioritized so the responsibilities which fall closest to home are taken care of first.

When several of our sons were in elementary school I became involved in Cub Scouts in order to join with them in the fun activities. As our program grew I became more and more active in the leadership until I was responsible for 110 little boys and their den leaders, plus remaining the den leader for my children. One night as I was running out the door for another meeting one of my sons said to me, "Mom, if you are doing all of this stuff for me, don't." His words stopped me dead in my tracks.

Have Child Sleep with Parents

One way to make sure children and parents spend the amount of time required together is to have the child sleep with the parents. Dr. William Sears in his book, <u>Nighttime Parenting</u> and Tine Thevenin in her book <u>The Family Bed</u>, discuss at length the numerous valuable connections which are made between parent and child when they sleep together.

Setting Family Tone

Proactive techniques involve creating a home environment and relationship with the children so being "respectful, responsible and fun to be around" is a desirable goal to the child. It is important to set a positive tone and make valued behaviors worthwhile. A high level of joy and enthusiasm is achieved by planning family activities, minimizing negatives and maximizing positives, knowing behavior will be repeated which gets the most attention.

Many aspects of maintaining a welcome family atmosphere are detailed in Delores Curran's book <u>Traits of a Healthy Family</u>. Curran details fifteen qualities commonly found in healthy families. While the families studied did not have the stressor of an emotionally problematic child, it is still an excellent tool in helping families assess themselves and find ways to capitalize on their strengths and minimize their weaknesses. The perfect family doesn't exist, but parents can improve their family setting so it is healthy for their children.

Tone of Voice

Part of creating a positive tone is speaking in loving ways and avoiding sarcasm and anger. After all, why would a child want to bond to someone who is irritable and belittling? Children need to learn to love their parent's voice. Talking and reading to the child in welcoming tones helps them become more receptive when discipline is necessary.

While there is a place for parental anger, for the most part, words spoken in anger or frustration push children deeper into themselves and away from their parents. When a parent is confronting a child on his lost coat in a biting tone the child is not thinking about where the coat is. The child is wondering how to get his parent out of his face, how long the harangue will last, and often, how to avoid the imminent blow. The parent is communicating, "I love you so much I don't want you to get cold." The child is hearing, "Mom hates me. The stupid coat is worth more to her than I am." It is better to use an appropriate reactive technique than to confuse the child by phrasing deep love and concern in harsh tones of criticism.

Clothing

Other forms of nurturing are important as well. Children need to look attractive in order to see a high regard reflected back to them from others. Unless someone close to the family is an excellent barber haircuts need to be professionally done. It is unfair for a child who needs to feel good about himself to look at his reflection in the mirror and see a chopped up embarrassment. Children also need nice clothes. Hand-me-downs and thrift store purchases can be used as part of a child's wardrobe when they are in good condition but nothing makes a child feel smarter and sharper than walking out of a store with brand-new, purchased-just-for-him by a parent investing the time and energy to shop just with him, new clothes. That does not mean a child can trash new clothes without the application of natural consequences, it just means there are times when new clothes are the best thing that could happen to a troubled child. The clear message the child gives to himself as he walks through life is, "I am worth looking this good."

Television

Another proactive trait is tight parental control of the television. Even good TV is bad for kids, particularly those with problematic behavior! Television is geared to the selling of products. The goal of the script writer is to gain viewers attention so they remain in their seats through the commercials. Whatever is going to keep people watching is what will be shown - regardless of the moral or violent tone of the images required. Yet, it is not merely the content of television programming that is the problem. It is the process of watching. The rapid fire images accustom children's eyes to stare intently at the same spot with the colors and shapes chosen for them by the camera. However, in order for children to learn to read their eyes must track from image to image. Rather than the information being shot effortlessly into the children's brains, reading requires the slow accumulation of skills and the application of imagination. Watching television is counterproductive to the development of both those skills.

To the child whose behavior is problematic, watching television creates yet another layer of distance between their parents and themselves. The TV does not relate. It does not answer questions or teach problem solving. Problems are presented and solved within thrity minutes, often with someone getting hurt in the process - definitely not reflective of real life! Children who are watching television are not relating to anyone. They are not engaging in reciprocal smiles, eye contact, movement or touch. None of the interactions essential to bonding and the development of healthy relationships are present. It does not need to be cut out of life altogether, however. Using the TV sparingly, as an occasional reward, when earned, gives children an incentive to work on their behavior. Even then, well-chosen movies tend to be better for children than commercial television programming.

We have a T.V. The children could be baking in the kitchen, playing basketball outside, assembling a puzzle, reading or otherwise engaged in a variety of worthwhile pursuits.

Somehow, the indiscernible click of the TV being turned on would resound through the house and one by one the kids stopped what they were doing and gravitated to the family room where they would sit entranced. When it became clear the TV was causing more problems than it was solving we decided to lock it up. An inexpensive money box was purchased and a metal fabricator punched a hole in one end which was big enough for the cord to fit through but too small for the plug. The plug was then locked into the box with the understanding that the T.V. would be available more selectively in the future. After several months the kids figured out how to pry open the box without unlocking it. When I discovered it I told them the lockbox was just a reminder of the house rule, they were still responsible for its enforcement. I then unplugged the TV and cut off the plug. The kids were speechless with surprise. It took them several days to figure out how to rewire it but I never had to use the lockbox again as they policed each other's use of the TV. They knew that if I cut the plug off again the cord would then be too short to reach from the set to the wall.

(For more information on the specific ways television hampers a child's personality development by stunting physical, emotional, and cognitive growth read my book <u>Even Good TV is Bad For Kids</u>.)

<u>Music</u>

Through the ages people have been aware of how mood is affected by music. While therapeutic parents would not get into any control battles over what music older children quietly listen to in their rooms, they often preempt the air space in the home with classical and harmonious sounds. In homes where children may attempt to take control by keeping the family in a high level of tension, calming music helps set a more desirable family tone.

Research done by Don Campbell, author of <u>The Mozart Effect,</u> clearly demonstrated that music by composers such as Mozart, Beethoven and Bach is therapeutic. Listening to it can activate parts of the brain and bring peace of mind. Various selections can be used to calm the over excited child or excite the depressed one. Campbell writes that in his experience, Mozart's violin concertos, especially numbers 3 and 4, produce strong positive effects on learning by strengthening the brain's processing capabilities.

Music can be incorporated in the home in numerous ways. Singing is good for the entire family. It is hard to be angry and destructive while singing as it causes a pleasurable resonation in the brain which counteracts and defeats negativity. Parents can sing silly songs as they wake their child up in the morning or call the family to meals. Families can sing songs along with the radio in the car or as they make dinner.

Spend several minutes each day toning as it has a powerful healing effect on the brain. According to Daniel Amen, author of <u>Change Your Brain, Change Your Life</u>, *Ahhh* evokes a relaxation response, *Eeee* aids concentration and releases pain and anger, and *Ohhh and Ommm* relaxes muscle tension.

Encourage the child to play a musical instrument.

After the family has seen a funny or pleasurable movie or attended a beautiful concert or musical, buy the tape or CD to it so the images can be replayed in the mind as the music arouses the memory. This suggestion is presupposing families are taking advantage of these events and making it a point to attend.

The bedrooms can have speakers in them which play appropriate music to the children as they fall asleep.

Rhythm

Moving in rhythmic ways aids brains which are chaotic and disorganized. Dancing and body movement is therapeutic as it enables the brain to reorganize itself and become wired along more useful pathways. In the home parents can get long flowing scarves for each member and everyone can participate in moving and dancing to the music. Rhythm instruments are always fun for small children as they march up and down and around to the beat in accompaniment to the music. Reading poetry and books such as those by Dr. Seuss lull a child's brain into following the rhythm and help them relax into the pulse picked by the parent. A commercially available device which fits over the eyes and ears can also be purchased. It is called a "Light and Sound" machine and is available through various psychotherapeutic magazines. Some children and their parents have found it wonderfully both energizing and relaxing as it bombards the eyes and ears with light and sound which affects the brain in deep reaching ways.

Encouragement

Proactive parents get excited whenever children are caught doing something right. Massive amounts of attention are not given to bad behavior. It is dealt with matter-of-factly, while the pizazz is saved for good behavior. For example, squealing with delight when children brush their teeth and ignoring it when they don't, focuses on the positives of their personality. Grabbing them up in a hug and swinging them around when they walk by other children without hitting them is worth an exclamation of joy and delight.

Parents may exclaim, "Wow, did you see what you just did? You walked by Jim without punching him!" or "Charlotte left her candy bar on the counter and it is still here! It is wonderful to know you are learning to respect her property."

Praising a child to others under the pretense the child is not listening enables children to hear positive words said about themselves without having to deflect them. Mother may exclaim to dad when the child is within hearing range, "Jeremy did the nicest thing today, he........."

Home Hygiene

Sometimes you don't need to be a better parent, you need to be a better housekeeper!

Children whose lives have been disrupted by the lack of structure inherent in moving from place to place and caretaker to caretaker are affected by disorganization. It is unrealistic to expect children who are emotionally and behaviorally chaotic to internalize a sense of order when they get up in the morning to a kitchen filled with the previous night's dirty dishes or come home after school to a living room cluttered with unsorted laundry. Working with a child, as opposed to continually leaving it to the child to do alone, to restore order in a home is a valuable therapeutic technique as it is a concrete way for children to symbolically address their psychological need for internal structure. When done with a loving parent it also provides an opportunity for bonding contact.

Personal Parental "Hygiene"

It is easy for parents to get so caught up in the child's behaviors and moods they fail to examine their own behaviors and moods and how they contribute to the child's state. Parents whose minds get locked into, "You will do it my way now," are just as much at fault as the child who says, "NO, NO, NO." When both the parent's brain and the child's brain shut down to other potential ways of resolving the conflict, the situation is a double whammy and can easily escalate to being out of control. The parent looks rigid and inflexible and the child looks oppositional defiant. Not all parent child relationships are based on what is called a "good fit". That is, the two personality styles are conflictual. Knowing what the parent's traits are which make it difficult for the child to create an "attached" relationship is important if the parent is going to be able to defuse the child's negative behaviors and not escalate them.

Anyone who has heard me lecture know I tend to talk very quickly. For most of our children this was not a problem. However, one son ended up completely shutting down at the sound of my voice. Processing what I said and the directions I gave was simply too exhausting and defeating for him. I interpreted his death defying refusals as oppositional-defiance and attachment disordered. As an adult he told me he was often just overwhelmed!

Frequently, it is not that the parent has a personality which is in conflict with the child, but the parent is exhausted and is not able to utilize the positive aspects of her personality to their best advantage. The more fatigued a parent is the less effective she is. Respite is critical to maintaining the high level of functioning required.

Respite can also help prevent the numerous side effects of stress – ulcers, Crohn's Disease, lupus, fybromyalgia, and cancers. These are all common to parents who are not taking good care of themselves. Even more common is being overweight. Mothers who do not get filled up through their relationship with their children, are instead drained. By the end of the day when they are exhausted and empty from giving and giving and giving, they tend to self-medicate with chocolate and other sugars. Parents must find ways to be supported and appreciated if they are going to avoid self-destructing under the pressures of nurturing their difficult children.

Chores

Chores make a child capable of taking care of himself. They build a sense of accomplishment and being needed. They teach the importance of reciprocity in relationships and help make the child appreciative of the work that parents put into running a home. In short, they are essential teaching tools for children to feel good about themselves and others. Children who don't do chores grow up believing someone else will always take care of their needs and life does not involve work. The problem with chores, however, is that teaching children how to do them requires a greater investment in time and energy on the part of the parent than will be immediately realized. Difficult children oftentimes need to be placed in the position of having to do something, and do it right, in order to give parents the opportunity to congratulate them on a job well-done. In the long run the parental positives given after the task will transfer to a willingness to do tasks for others, ie. teachers and employers. Initially, however, the results will not be worthwhile so long term commitment to the realization of future goals must be kept in mind.

Teaching children how to do chores requires three elements. One is the understanding on the part of the parents that the issue in doing chores is not just in getting a task done or achieving compliance. The issue is about trust, connectedness and where the child fits in life. Therefore the bonding elements of eye contact, touch, movement and food need to be present and pizazzy in order for the child to connect doing chores to loving and being loved.

The second element of teaching chores requires a foundation in consequencing skills. There is no point in asking a child to do something if there is no plan of what is going to happen when the child doesn't do it.

The third element involves planning. Initially doing chores must be fun for the child and fun for the parent. As the child gets older the parent gradually is removed and more and more of the chore is done by the child, there is less and less an expectation of fun and more an expectation of taking personal responsibility to do one's share of the work involved in running a home.

Teaching my daughter to do the dishes by herself after a meal took five years to accomplish. When we adopted her at four she occasionally helped by standing on a stool in front of the kitchen sink, playing in the soapy water while rinsing the dishes prior to being loaded in the dishwasher. As she got older we did not leave it to her to volunteer to rinse the dishes but assigned her one evening a week when it was her turn to help. By the time she was five she did not play so much, rather she took it as a matter of course that one night a week she needed to rinse the dishes. She could play if she wanted, it didn't matter how it was done or how long it took as long as the results met expectations. The foundation of expectation had been laid. By the time she was six she was helping to clear the table and rinse. Later, loading the dishwasher was added. There was a gradual introduction of new tasks. At eight she was helping to clear the table, put items away, rinse the dishes, load and unload the dishwasher, wiping the counters, cleaning the sinks and sweeping the kitchen. She was not working alone yet, there was still a family member helping. Sometime during her ninth year she was asked to do it alone intermittently. Doing it by herself, one evening a week, became the norm several months later.

This process can be shortened considerably, and possibly even eliminated, with older children but the elements remains the same. In some way there needs to be some form of pleasure or reward injected into the chore. Parents must model doing chores themselves, occasionally working alongside the child. Consequences need to be available to ensure the task is completed so the child can earn approval for a job well done. Parents must keep in mind the chore is a means to an end, not the end. The goal is not chore completion but growth in the child's ability to love himself and others and to demonstrate that love with reciprocity.

When having a child do chores the distinction between compliance and cooperation is helpful to understand. Cooperation comes from a deep willingness of the heart, compliance just means getting the unwanted task done. It is wonderful when children cooperate with doing chores out of sense of joy and fulfillment. However, since cooperation is a higher level concept for many children we settle for compliance, hoping the sense of cooperation will develop as the child matures and learns to trust and love. Compliance is indicated by the attitude, "I don't want to do it and I'm going to do it anyway." Having the child verbalize that sentiment when asked to do a chore can help to break down the resistance and allows the parent to acknowledge how hard it is for the child to do what is being asked and to express appreciation for the child's efforts. "I know how hard it is to help out when you don't want to. Mopping the floor is a dirty job. I want you to know I really appreciate your help and am glad you are learning to do things you don't want to do. That is a tough skill even for adults."

Work does not have to be done with a good attitude. By doing chores, even when they don't want to, in an acceptable frame of mind, parents model for their children that chores are simply a part of life. It gives them an excellent opportunity for them to demonstrate it is possible to have negative feelings and handle them well. It also teaches children to look past the unpleasant parts of the task to the joy of completion and the rewards which follow - play time, ice cream, picnic, money. No one works for free, even volunteers get some form of reward for their efforts. Adults hold jobs in order to get the pay at the end of the month. Children are no different. They must have an expectation of something good happening when their work is all done if they are to buy into the concept that doing chores well will ultimately work out well for them.

Avoid the Tyranny of Time

Very few things in life have to be done the moment they are thought of. Most people, children and adults, even when they don't mind doing something, object to being told it must be done immediately. To children whose approach to life is negative, "Now" is a four letter word and must be avoided. When making a request it is often possible to give some latitude as to the time line or ask the child when it would be convenient for him to get it done. Asking, "When is a good time for you to take out the trash?" or "Before you come to the dinner table please see that the trash is taken out." has the potential to sometimes yield a better response then, "Take the trash out now."

Changing Family Tone

Despite a parent's best efforts there will be times when everyone in the house is tense and ill-tempered. Those times can be minimized by a parent determined to not let a negative mood infect the entire day and pervade the atmosphere. Rather than homing in on the child causing the most disturbance it is often helpful to gather everyone together in an activity consciously designed to lighten the mood. For some reason, ordering pizza is a guaranteed mood lifter. Parents may be perfectly capable of making an excellent pizza from scratch, at home, for half the price. However, there is something magical and mystical about having pizza delivered to the door which says, "Let's party!"

Making cookie dough is another sure-fire way to lift spirits. Note, the point is not to bake cookies, the point is to make cookie dough.   Any dough which is not eaten with the fingers and actually makes it into the oven to be baked does not count. The concern for the therapeutic parent is not cavities in their children's teeth, which any good dentist can fix, but holes in their children's hearts, which only they can fix. (If the dough is going to be eaten raw don't add eggs.) Fingerpainting with catsup on the refrigerator, taking a long walk, reading out loud, playing a non-competitive board game or game of cards are all good ways to change tone.   Creativity and the willingness to be unorthodox are essential to turning frowns into smiles.

It is important that parents not always get caught up in techniques which consequence, force a sense of responsibility, and cause thoughtfulness in the children. Sometimes it is appropriate to just lighten up and have a good time. After all, children spend more time in relationship with their parents as adults than they do as children. They need to have a memory bank full of good times which will glue them together as a family long after they have left home.

<u>Rituals</u>

That memory bank is often filled with the rituals which a family engaged in. It doesn't take much to create a family ritual. Baking cookies once at Christmas causes children to say at every Christmas thereafter, "We <u>always</u> bake cookies at Christmas."   Such is the importance to children of predictability and stability.   Children who have come from previous family experiences which left them looking at the world as an unfriendly, dangerous place need help seeing the world as predictably positive.   Rituals, by fixing in the child's memory a certain positive event will occur at the same time each day, week, month or year, enable children to look forward to the future with pleasure instead of hopelessness.

Reading to a child every night before bedtime, brushing a child's hair each morning, attending worship every week, singing a certain song when a child is blue enables a child to feel hopeful for the future. Knowing the first of school will be greeted with new pencils and new clothes gives a child a new outlook that this year will be better.

Due to previous abuse issues of most of our children and the understanding that for some of them the abuse occurred primarily at night or was somehow connected to the dark, we consciously strove to surround bedtime with a sense of warmth and safety. We made it a predictable calm routine of baths, teeth brushing, getting into pajamas, bringing a stuffed animal or blanket into the living room and reading aloud. The first books read were generally funny and entertaining. Sometimes, we would read a little poetry. <u>Jabberwocky</u> by

Lewis Carroll and illustrated by Graeme Base was a favorite. It and the book we tended to finish with, <u>Goodnight Moon</u> by Margaret Brown were both memorized by most of the children. From the day after Thanksgiving to when the children went back to school after Christmas our large collection of Christmas books were shared each evening.

Following reading time the children went to their rooms to get into bed. We would then go from room to room, bed to bed, sitting on the edge, talking quietly for a few minutes, hearing concerns of the day, plans for tomorrow, blessing, hugging and kissing each other in the quiet ritual of love. Lights were turned out as we left, however bedroom doors were always left open so light would shine in and the children could hear us continue to talk or move quietly through the house as they relaxed their vigil and nodded off to sleep.

Holidays are known by their rituals and there is a reason why adult children come home for them. They come home because there are certain events during the year which have become surrounded with massive amounts of rituals and they want to re create the enjoyable times of their childhood and share those times with their spouse and children. They want to link the joys of the past to the joys of the present and establish a foundation of joy for the future.

Family rituals fill that need. Parents do their families a disservice when they get so caught up in the negative behavior of the children they neglect the creation of family rituals.

Holiday Blues

Although most families associate the holiday seasons with warm memories, for many children holidays are a source of stress. Halloween may not mean dress up and candy. It may mean satanic rituals. Christmas may bring memories of deprivation and threats of not being good enough to deserve presents. The anticipation of New Year's Eve or Super Bowl Sunday may be coupled with thoughts of drunkenness and abuse. Parents need to be sensitive to these ghosts in their children's past and understand why behavior may deteriorate around holidays. Putting a child's history on a timeline can be a useful way to look for cyclical behaviors which coincide with the last time they saw their birth mother or the day their dog died. When a child can have it graphically explained to him there is a reason he is feeling or acting the way he is he can use that information to minimize the negative effects.

Reciprocal Relationships

Because unattached children are, by definition, self-centered and self-dependent for everything, developing reciprocal relationships is part of the therapeutic parenting process.

Therapeutic parents must provide many opportunities for disturbed children to interact in a reciprocal way.

Learning to trust others to take care of them, take comfort in being cared for, and to take care of others in return, is essential to success. Participating in joint activities, doing chores and paying back those they injure through their thoughtlessness are all learning tasks of the unattached child.

Particularly important is making sure siblngs are taken care of when a child hurts them or destroys their property. This allows the children to maintain a good working relationship between them. To allow the build up of a wall of resentment to occur between the children who injure and the children who are in some way injured destroys morale in a family. Children need to know they will be taken care of when their brother or sister misbehaves at their expense so they can forgive and move on with the relationship.

The bottom line is, "The victim decides". It is not up to the child who wrecked havoc to determine the value to the victim of the destroyed property or the amount of pain experienced. It is up to the child who has been hurt to decide what needs to be done to make up for or counteract the ill will generated by the misdeed. The victim can request a toy be handed over in exchange for the destroyed one, a victim's chore be done by the perpetrator to make up for the hurt, a dessert handed over to compensate for the embarrassment to friends, etc. The victim needs to be counseled, however, that to extract too great a penalty will cause resentment and the need to seek further vengence. Responsibility for the behavior will be enhanced while escalation of the behavior will be avoided if there is a sense of equity between what was done and what needs to happen to make up for it.

A child continually made demeaning comments to his sister regarding her race, her size, her sexuality and anything else he could to arouse her ire. Finally she had had enough and decided a pay-back was required for the humiliation he caused her in front of her friends and when she was alone. It was negotiated that he would do her dishes for her the next time it occurred. That was all it took. It stopped immediately as our daughter would walk up to him and say, "I don't want to do the dishes tonight because I have made plans with friends. Could you please say something ugly to me right now so I can leave after dinner?"

Oxygen Intake - Yours and Your Child's

During crises the parents' ability to control their own level of arousal is often the only factor standing between a rationally based and an emotionally based resolution to an event. In fact several studies indicate a child's response to an event is often dependent on the response of trusted adults. It is therefore important for adults to not determine their child's reaction by their own overreaction.

Conscious breathing, practiced for centuries by those engaged in a variety of spiritual disciplines, develops control of one's own level of arousal. Practitioners of Yoga, Buddhism, Christian meditation and other disciplines know that breathing is the core to focusing on a calm center inside oneself. Focusing on one's center is key to staying aloof from the emotional storms of others and remaining impassive can keep a situation from escalating.

The marvel of quietly taking control of one's breathing is not that responses to a situation are then limited. Rather, they are expanded to include a wide variety of choices which were previously eliminated when the first impulse was the only one available. A loud, abrasive tone of voice could still be chosen if the parent felt it was warranted, for example, as in a One-Minute Scolding. A harsh look could still be chosen for the face and a stiff body posture could still be affected. However, the basic rule for anger is that the more angry you are the quieter you need to speak. The more upset you are the softer the demeanor you need to reflect in order to avoid a "fight or flight" response from automatically engaging in the child. By using the space in and between the breaths to think many more options are accessed.

Just as in the Lamaze training for birthing mothers, the time to learn measured breathing techniques is not after the baby is in the birth canal and the pain becomes overwhelming. The time to practice is prior to the critical need. In the same way, the time to learn breath control is when there is no parent-child crisis. By regularly engaging in a discipline which involves focusing on the breathing process parents have a unique tool at their disposal whenever the occasion requires it.

As I worked on these thoughts the computer began to do weird things like deleting lines, double printing lines and not allowing the cursor to go where it was put. In a panic I called out to my son, "Matthew, help, the computer is going crazy. I am going to lose this chapter!" He calmly came over and said slowly and deliberately, "Now... Mother.... breathe... take it easy... move back from the computer." I did so. He made a few key strokes and stepped away. When I asked him what he did to fix it he said, "I remained calm."

Conscious breathing is equally important to children. When a child is about to attempt a difficult task, such as following a parent directive to hand over a note from the school, smiling and telling the child to breathe deeply, deflects the child's rising sense of alarm and allows a clearer thinking process to kick in. By the same token, after a child has done something well, telling him to take a deep breath fills him with an expanded sense of well-being over his accomplishment and cannot help but make him stand straighter and his face light up with a smile. By engaging the child's entire body in the feeling of good will it is more deeply internalized.

During cuddle times a deeper connectedness occurs when the parent's and the child's breathing is in unison. One way to accomplish that is to bring the child in close and then match his breathing. As the parent slowly deepens and elongates her breathing the receptive child's breathing will also deepen and stretch out until a deeper state of relaxation within the safety and nurturance of the parent's arms occurs.

Being able to take control of one's own breathing and effect the breathing of a child to effect a relaxed state in the face of crisis is not an easy ability to develop, but for the therapeutic parent, the discipline required is well worth the effort.

Attend Worship

While it is advantageous when parents believe in the tenets of a particular faith and desire to worship regularly in order to reinforce their belief system, faith is not necessary. Attending worship services is valuable even without "believing". Most worship incorporates numerous elements which are very healthy for children and families. Getting a family up at the same time, eating together, and out the door together once a week is very helpful for family organization. When the family then goes out for breakfast together afterwards there is an added bonus. One family has sweet rolls on Sunday after church which are not offered any other day. This connects going to church with the pleasure centers of the brain.

Jim Mahoney, a therapist in Spokane Washington tells this story at this workshops:

When he was a young therapist just starting out in practice he began work with a particularly difficult family. He saw the members separately and in small groups and then decided he needed to see them all together at the same time every week. They agreed to meet every Wednesday from 5 – 6 p.m. After their session it was too late to go home to fix dinner so they would eat out. The family dynamics began to dramatically improve. Jim went on vacation for two weeks and regretfully told the family he would have to miss those appointments. The family went to dinner anyway while he was gone and to everyone's surprise continued to make excellent progress. When Jim returned he discovered, much to his chagrin, it was the family going out to dinner together which was enabling their progress. Not just his work!

Attending worship on Sunday together accomplishes much the same thing. Everyone in the family is organized around meeting a common goal which helps the family work as a cohesive unit rather than separate parts.

Additional benefits of participating in the worship life of a community is the music and the positive message. The messages tend to focus on the need for reciprocal, loving behaviors and meeting the human justice needs of the world. Forgiveness and how it heals both the abused and the abuser is also a theme which children who have been hurt by their previous parents need to hear. Listening to morally sound, positive, uplifting messages once a week is beneficial in and of itself. During worship the children learn to follow the lead of someone other than their parents. They learn to sit quietly when others sit and stand when others stand. They learn there are arenas in life where running, talking and noise making are not allowed. During the hymns parents can place their finger on the line of the music so the child can follow along. The child learns how to read and memorize in a non-threatening environment which has no tests.

The fellowship involved in the community is very helpful to parents who often have few places to turn for non-judgemental, unqualified, support and understanding. Adolescents, particularly, need an adult, who is not their parent, to talk to and spend time with. Many worshipping communities provide such an adult as part of their youth ministry. Getting the troubled adolescent together with other teens under the supervision of a youth worker can be very beneficial in creating a support group for the teen which he might not have access to at school or through other arenas because his negative reputation has preceded him.

Younger children need the same thing. Often children who act out at school and at home do well for the short time they are expected to in church. Their good behavior is reflected in the esteem which others, who do not know how they behave otherwise, give them. They get to practice being "good" and seeing how it feels. Parents can see how well their child is capable of behaving and set realistic goals for them.

People to help with respite can also be frequently identified within the fellowship. Most religious communities have programs for children and youth which are extremely healthy for them to participate in. While the children are positively engaged, the parents can take advantage of the much needed respite. Summer camps associated with faith communities tend to be less expensive to attend and often carpooling is provided to get the children to and from camp. When finances are an issue often other members of the community will donate what is needed.

Search Institute, an organization devoted to research regarding the state of America's youth, has discovered that adolescents who participate in a worshipping community on a regular basis are more apt to lead healthy life styles and reject premarital sex, smoking and drugs. They are less apt to engage in delinquent behaviors and more apt to be successful in school. It is significant to note that after the shootings at Columbine High School in Littleton, Colorado in the spring of 1999, the students flocked to the local churches, not the counseling staff set up and trained to provide crisis and grief services. Even those youth who did not consider themselves to be religious went to the churches alone and with their friends as they found such a high degree of comfort and support there.

Memory Bank Deposits and Withdrawals

Children who have been hurt as infants tend to focus on the pain of those early years rather than the pleasure of the present. Memories can trigger emotional releases similar to those which occurred with the actual event. When a child's brain continually replays the hurts of the past the same emotional responses are replayed as well. They cannot stop replaying those memories unless they have other memories which override them. The positive memories need to have just as much emotional impact as the hurtful ones. If the abuse involved a great deal of movement then amusement rides and roller coasters might be what is needed to supplant them.

Overriding the impact of the early abuse and neglect on the scarred brain takes conscious effort. Parents need to regularly plan and participate in fun events with their children in order to override those memories. Special events need to be commemorated with photographs, ticket stubs and programs. (Videos are not as useful as the images are not constantly available.) Somewhere in the home or in the child's bedroom where it is frequently seen a bulletin board needs to be devoted to displaying the momentos of the fun times. The events can be referred to at dinner or at bedtime when family time can be devoted to asking, "What was the most fun thing you remember about this week/last month/Christmas/summer vacation?" "What do you remember seeing/smelling/wearing/doing?" "Who was present?" The events need to be described in such a way that a memory of it is firmly implanted with as many details as can be recalled. The fun times need to be revisited again and again in order to rewire the brain for pleasure instead of pain.

Physical Exercise

It is difficult to maintain a negative mood or affect while the body is engaged in exercise. Families who take long walks in the evening, bike ride together, go swimming, and participate in other physical activities together have a mechanism to elevate both the individual and collective mood in the family. Exercise provides people with a higher level of enthusiasm and joy and prevents feelings of lethargy. It increases metabolism, eliminates or slows weight gain and enhances sleep. Exercise increases blood flow to the brain and speeds up the rate of healing. People who exercise often find they need less medication to achieve the same anti-depressant results. Children who participate in regular exercise do better in organized sports activities in school and have higher self-esteem. With all these benefits parents whose children are brain damaged due to early abuse and neglect cannot afford to pass by the healthful, healing properties of exercising with their children. And it really comes down to that. Exercise is not something a parent can order a child to do. If it is to be effective and promote family and parent bonding, it is best when everyone finds an activity that all can enjoy and they regularly participate in it together.

Issues Outside the Home - School & Community
<u>School Issues</u>

The separation of home and school is invaluable when building a bonded relationship with a child. Children who have experienced a fairly normal development benefit from having parents who are present in school and, depending on what is developmentally appropriate, actively involved in the child's education. This is not necessarily true for children whose relationship with their parents is problematic and who could actively work to cause a split between the parents and the teachers. When parents are stretched to the limit trying to maintain a child in their home it is not realistic for them to additionally monitor homework and be continually called to the school to discuss discipline problems. It is far better for the parents to directly say to the child and the school, "Good luck, hope you can work it out. If you can't, fourth grade will also be available again next year." School performance is a child's issue and to make it the parent's issue can confuse the bonding work. If necessary, it can be made clear in the child's IEP (Individual Education Plan) that "parental involvement is not expected and will be counterproductive to the child's educational goals. All homework will be done under the supervision of a teacher or teacher's aide at school."

As we told one son, "As long as you are stealing it is OK for you to choose to flunk school. The world does not need smart thieves."

The child's potential behaviors must be shared with the school in advance and parents can help the school by discussing what consequences will be endorsed and what won't, and what tends to work and what doesn't. Letting the school know the parents can be called in as a resource is different than allowing the school to have the expectation that problems which arise at school, regarding behaviors, homework or grades, will be automatically consequenced by the already struggling parents.

In exasperation I once sweetly said to my son's teacher, "I tell you what, when you are having difficulty coping with my son's behavior at school or getting him to stay on task I will be glad to come over and help out as long as when I am having trouble coping with his behavior at home because he is fighting with his brother or won't do his chores I can call you and you will come over and help out."

A parent can be a valuable resource to the school by supporting any consequence the school decides is appropriate. Generally the parents are supportive of more severe consequences than the school would consider, but there are times when a consequence can be negotiated and even a few rare times when the parents can volunteer to enforce the consequence.

During a particularly difficult week with one of our children - after running away, foul language, refusal to do work and other angry behaviors not typical of second graders - his teacher called home to ask for suggestions. We agreed to "fire him" from school. We explained to him, "Everybody has a job. Daddy has a job earning the money to pay for our food and home. I have a job keeping everything at home running smoothly. The teacher has a job educating the children in her classroom. Your job is to learn to read and write. There are times, however, when people just don't seem to be capable of doing their job and when that happens they can be fired. If Daddy doesn't do what he needs to do for his company than his company can say, 'We don't need you anymore' and so can fire him. People who do not learn to read and write can be fired from jobs which require reading and writing and then taught to do jobs which they can do with their hands. So, next time you decide you do not want to do the work of reading and writing your teacher is going to fire you and send you home where I will teach you how to clean the stove, wash the refrigerator and learn other jobs which do not require reading and writing." The next time he acted out in school and was clearly not contributing to his own or anyone else's learning the teacher "fired him" and I came and got him. He worked the rest of the day on chores at home. The next week he needed to try the behaviors again and was then "fired" for three days. That was the last time the consequence needed to be used.

This consequence worked with the parent enforcing it because the parent had already established a relationship with the child. When that is not present than the child needs to be fired to a foster home or day care where the foster or day care mother is present to teach the chores and enforce the consequence. At the end of the school day the child would then go home, regardless of the state of the required chores, to return the next day and the next until compliance had been demonstrated.

Working with schools on discipline and performance issues is easier when the school sees the parents as allies. Volunteering to help with fund raisers and aiding in the library are ways for parents to support the school while not interacting directly with their own child. The more school staff sees the parent as an asset to the school the more willing they are to work with them to problem solve issues regarding the child.

Community Issues

While parents can legitimately leave school issues to the school to handle that is not the case with community issues. Parents need to demonstrate to their children and to the police they are on the front line with law enforcement officials and will fully cooperate with them. Sometimes that means parents must be the first to call police when their children commit an illegal act. The family and child will get more fair and respectful treatment from the police and the courts when they know the family is doing all it can to establish a sense of law and order in the child. To protect a child from the legal consequences of their behavior is to set the child up to behave illegally again and the family up to be disrespected in the community for adopting children who prey on their neighbors and drain the communities resources.

An acquaintance called and said, "I think I just saw your son climb out the window of the house next door." The police were immediately called and they were at our home within minutes of the time our son walked in the door, allowing them to confront him and catch him with the stolen items still on him. Another time a son came home with a bleeding arm and an unusual story of how it happened. After we went to the emergency room for stitches I called the police and said, "My son has just gotten stitches in his arm. It looks like he gashed it on broken glass. If anyone calls to report an incident of breaking and entering let me know." The next day an officer called and said the school had been broken into and there was blood on the floor.

The boys learned from these incidents if they get involved in illegal behavior we will cooperate totally with law enforcement. The police and community residents have learned we can be depended on to support them in their efforts and they may call us any time they see our children act suspiciously or they have reason to believe any of our children were involved in a delinquent or illegal act. We will not rescue or make excuses for them.

The down side is the ire we arouse in other parents whose children are with ours when an illegal act is committed. We have been heatedly told, "You turn your children into the police, but don't you dare turn in ours!" Our stance has also angered our children as they have had to do community service hours, pay restitution and even go to a juvenile lock-up while their compatriots experienced no consequence as a result of their actions because their parents hired a lawyer and got them off.

Nonetheless, we remain committed to the belief that our children and society will benefit from our totally cooperative stance with the police and a little "confinement therapy" may be just what a child needs to give thought to the direction of their life.

Professional and Therapeutic Inventions
Accurate Diagnosis and Medication

The more research is devoted to exploring the roots of negative behaviors the more clear it becomes that the study of emotional and behavioral disturbance is a study of how abuse and neglect damage the brain and cause it to misinterpret events and direct courses of action which are not healthy. The brain has been inured and the negative pattern of behaviors is the result. Brain scans of people who are highly anxious, violent, compulsive, etc show unmistakable, irregular patterns. They show activity where there should not be any and black holes where there should be activity. The brains can look like cottage cheese where they should be smooth and have holes where there should be connections. Some of the damage can be genetic. For instance, a parent who is hyperactive with poor impulse control may show a particular brain pattern which is replicated in the child. Other brain damage can be the result of a blow to the head so an individual who was mild mannered before a car accident is irritable afterwards. Other damage is the result of an early environment characterized by pervasive abuse and neglect. Regardless of how the brain was injured, it is the brain which must be healed if specific behaviors are to be changed.

Healing the brain must be approached from numerous directions. Parenting interventions, nutrition, physical activity, and the other ideas suggested in this book each contribute in their own way to brain growth and development, help to heal the brain injury and positively affect the negative patterns of behavior. Not to be overlooked is medication. Just as an individual with diabetes takes insulin to stay alive, certain medications are necessary for the injured brain to function optimally. Knowing which medications help which conditions is the function of an experienced and trained psychiatrist.

Not all psychiatrists make medication management their specialty so it is important the right doctor be identified. Too often, patients are directed to a psychiatrist, not because that doctor is the best and can optimize the medication management, but because he will take Medicaid. Valuable time and energy is wasted while parents, who often know more about their child's condition than the doctor does, are not listened to by the psychiatrist. The staff psychiatrist who is excellent at treating adult depression may be at a loss when faced with a child with reactive attachment disorder. It is like a doctor who is adept at brain surgery being called in to operate on the heart.

Dr. John Alston, an expert in the field of psychotropic medications for childhood behavioral and emotional disturbances, has written a chart to help parents differentiate between a few of the more common diagnosis associated with negative patterns of behavior. He also suggests medications which he has found to be useful in addressing those issues. His chart is found in the section titled "Attachment Symptoms and Differential Diagnosis", page 64. Another valuable resource is Dr. Amen's book, Change Your Brain, Change Your Life.

Chiropractic and Acupuncture

The goal of both of these medical interventions is restoring and maintaining the body's balance. Unfortunately they are often not covered by insurance. Nonetheless, spinal adjustments and applying stimulation to key nerve endings and body points can have both short term and long term benefits to children whose negative behaviors and mood are unstable and out of control.

Nutrition and Diet

One of the indicators of a child not willing or able to take in his parents love is his rejection of his mother's cooking. When a child always wants to eat out, it is a sign the attachment is stressed. Refusing to eat the food his mother lovingly prepares is a way for him to refuse to let her love and nurturing in.   Food, well prepared, is essential to a home environment. One of the tools of a home where parents take seriously the job of creating a healing environment is a breadmaking machine. For children to walk in after school to the smell of fresh bread is like walking into heaven. Even the most callous child cannot reject the aroma of "something lovin from the oven" and keep it from searing his brain with love. In order for these loving smells to sneak into a child's brain they must originate in the kitchen. Home cooked meals fill the home with "aromatherapy".   Cinnamon tends to particularly arouse feelings of good will.

Optimally families will eat together. Sharing good food and good times creates a sense of the whole familiy, instead of separate parts living under the same roof.

Caffiene is a culprit and damages brain development by constricting the flow of blood to the brain. While it serves as a stimulant in the short run, the long term effect is the brain needs more and more to achieve the desired effect. The more consumed the more tired the child ultimately feels. The caffiene in the soft drink thus immediately satisfies the craving while creating a long term need for more stimulation.

Vitamin, herbal, mineral and food supplements can have a beneficial effect and must not be overlooked in the search for helpful tools to aid healing. It is helpful to explore the issues which a particular child is experiencing and see which supplements minimize or maximize the emotional state desired. Valerian root and kava extract, for example, are herbal supplements frequently used to calm anxiety and help produce a deep, relaxing sleep in children and adults. Chamomile tea and the B vitamins are also helpful. Gingko biloba is often used to increase blood flow to the brain and helps with energy, focusing and impulse control. St. John's Wort is sometimes as effective an anti-depressant as a medication. A good resource for additional ways to address behavioral and mood disorders with nutrition and supplements is Prescription for Nutritional Healing by James and Phyllis Balch. Any supplement used must be first cleared with the child's physician.

Aromatherapy

Numerous scents are useful to enhance relaxation or other mental states. The oil from lavender flowers is particularly used to help people feel less stressed and depressed. A little on the pillow at night helps children relax and go to sleep. A good guide to other herbs with healing properties is The Complete Medicinal Herbal by Penelope Ody. (Essential aromatherapy oils are not to be ingested!)

Choosing a Therapist and Therapeutic Intervention

Some children, depending on their emotional and behavioral issue respond well to Play Therapy, others to Developmental Play Therapy or Theraplay. These interventions are not the same and do not the have the same results with all children. Some children show marked improvement with Bio-Feedback, Dance Therapy or Sand Tray Therapy, Still others are helped by the insight based therapies, where talking is the norm. Among the numerous therapies which have been known to help children there is none more controversial than Holding Therapy. This therapy has many proponents and detractors, yet must be carefully explored before it is chosen or rejected. Typically, professional mental health workers (doctors, social workers, psychotherapists) are among the detractors of the therapy. Meanwhile parents who live with the disturbed child have not been able to get help until they turned to holding therapy and so are avid cheer leaders for the intervention. All of the therapeutic interventions depend as much on the skill, philosophical bent and experience of the practitioner as on the method of intervention.

What is important is that parents whose children are behaviorally and emotionally challenging need to seek help, for their child's sake as well as their own. That help should not be chosen based on the comfort level of the parents and other adult decision makers, but on the effectiveness with the child. To take a child to play therapy or insight based therapy week after week, month after month, year after year, while the child's behaviors deteriorate, because it is the treatment of choice for the mental health center or social worker or because the therapist will take Medicaid is a form of abuse and neglect. Results don't lie and it is results children need.

(See the chapter "Holding Therapies – Harmful, or Rather Beneficial" in my book titled For What It's Worth.)

Techniques On the Line Between Pro-active and Reactive

A few reminders of some basics:

The <u>pro-active approach</u> is used to avoid problems and encourage positive behavior.
The <u>re-active approach</u> is used as a response to negative behavior.

And:

Rules #1, #2, & #3: Always take good care of yourself!

Somewhere in and among these basic concepts falls the essential element of family safety. It is not always necessary, and indeed, is sometimes foolish, to wait for something to happen in order to formulate an appropriate response. With many children, particularly those with more severe behavioral symptoms, it is best to read the child's history and assume the worst case scenario adjustment pattern. That means rather than waiting for the child to pick a time and place to cause physical, emotional or personal damage, as soon as he arrives he is within the viewing area of an adult at all times and at night is placed in a bedroom with some form of alarm system on the door.

Many parents have protested this is tantamount to declaring a child guilty and punishing him before he has done anything. Right! All children need to feel safe. Those already living in the home and those entering the home have a paramount need for security. Children cannot heal emotional wounds when they are continually needing to assess their surroundings. Better by far to make it clear to everyone that as long as this adult is in charge no one needs to be afraid of getting hurt or having their possessions stolen than to miscalculate and trust a child who is untrustworthy. If that means children need to be in compliance with the tightest supervision and then earn their way to looser supervision, than so be it.

Another protest comes from parents concerned about how being monitored by an alarm negatively affects the child's self esteem. When forthrightly confronted children tend to have a realistic view of the damage they can do while sneaking around. They often understand more than their parents do the necessity of the alarm. Rather than have their self esteem damaged they realize more damage would be done to their sense of self if they were allowed to roam about at will and endanger themselves, the home or their family. To allow a child to be destructive sets in place a negative view of themselves and their power to destroy which far out weighs any ego damage done by their confinement.

This approach has benefits for everyone. The child being supervised minute by minute during the day and monitored at night by an alarm system learns that not only will he not hurt anyone, but no one can hurt him either. If he can't get out of his room without setting off an alarm, than no one can come in! Additionally, it is hard enough to create working relationships without the added problems created by possessions getting broken or disappearing. Keeping a child closely on track means he will have less damage to be consequenced around. He will be able to create friends in the home without first making enemies of them. Lastly, a new child in the home is often the one accused when something is broken or missing. With an alarm system there is less chance of false accusations being lodged against him.

The rest of the family benefits because they can sleep more secure and be more relaxed in their own home knowing someone, somehow is monitoring the child.

Most of the therapeutic parents I know get their alarms through Radio Shack. They come in a wide variety of styles and are relatively inexpensive. Some attach to the door frame or door and are activated when the door opens. Others are placed in such a way as to be activated when the child breaks a light beam or when movement occurs outside an accepted area. Different children respond differently to different systems. When there is more than one child in a bedroom or when a child is destructive to himself or the objects in the room it might be better to not use a system dependent on the door being closed.

In order to avoid being held hostage by the child routinely, deliberately setting off the alarm requiring a parent to come running, the child must be aware that an appropriate consequence will be assigned the next day every time the alarm is activated.

Reactive Parenting Techniques

Despite the best efforts of the best parents children will continue to act in negative, inappropriate ways. When children do not take advantage of the enjoyment life and the family have to offer and make poor behavior choices, then it is necessary to react and find various ways of demonstrating "sad for" the child, rather than "mad at" the child in a manner that is not punitive, but allows both the parent and child to have a "win-win" experience.

There are a variety of techniques to accomplish this. Deciding which one to use is one of experimentation. One thought to keep in mind when choosing is to reason with the child when he is being reasonable and take action with the child when the child is being governed by emotions. Another key thought is the foundation of discipline is creating and maintaining the right relationship with your child, not using the right techniques.

<u>Philosophy of Parenting</u>

The therapeutic parents believe:

"You can do the wrong thing over and over, or, you can do the right thing once!"

When a technique has been tried several times and has not achieved a desired behavior change, the parent modifies it. Because techniques are continually being changed, the parents have developed a wide repertoire of responses to negative behavior. Positive behaviors forced upon children are not internalized as well as those they choose to adopt with therapeutic parental nudging, so the goal is to create thoughtfulness in the child so the child chooses to change.   Most people do not change their behavior until the price gets to be too high to continue it. Creating situations where the price for maintaining a behavior is high, and the reward for changing the behavior is equally high, is the goal.

The reactive techniques, used to interrupt, redirect, and/or correct poor behavior, can be seen as a continuum, ranging from non-intrusive (ignoring behavior) to extremely instrusive (one-minute scolding), with the least intrusive form of intervention always being the first choice. The techniques are generally used without warning in order to avoid a build up of resistance. Underpinning all reactive discipline techniques is a firm foundation of consequencing, which is to have children experience either a real-world or similar to a real-world consequence to their behavior. Consequencing as a parenting technique is dealt with further in <u>Parenting With Love and Logic</u> and <u>Parenting Teens With Love and Logic</u>, both by Foster Cline and Jim Fay.

<u>Power Struggles</u>

Pivotal to understanding consequencing is differentiating between which behaviors are worth controlling and which ones are not. The child's unspoken job is to get the parents. The parents job is to not get got. Avoiding control battles, especially those which cannot be won, is essential if children are going to listen to and respect parental authority. Therapeutic parents, therefore, do not attempt to control:

> food intake
> hygiene issues
> choice of friends
> hairstyles, etc.

They believe you "take it all, you lose it all", so they willingly give away the control they don't need and they don't have anyway.

Rule Number One of avoiding control battles is to pick the issue very carefully, because Rule Number Two is, once it is picked, it must be won. To give in to a child on an issue which is important to the parents entrenches the negative brain pattern in the child and makes positive behavior and cooperation in the future even more difficult.

Being relentlessly persistent in the face of relentless provocation, while maintaining a sense of lightness, grace and humor is the mark of a great parent.

One time honored way to avoid control battles is to change the rules. When the parent makes the rules, the parent can change the rules. The rules can be changed through negotiation or they can be changed by decree. Negotiation demonstrates a willingness on the part of the parent to be fair and an ability to reexamine constantly changing situations. To enter into negotiations with a child teaches the art of compromise and models getting to "yes" without hostility.

It is essential, however, the parents not capitulate in order to avoid a control battle which must be one. Those are respect for parents and family environment. Children must learn to do their chores and help out around the house and they must treat their parents with respect. These are not negotiable.

Many children with oppositional and defiant personality characteristics get into control battles because the adrenalin rush it produces in their brains is stimulating. There is nothing they enjoy more than a good fight. It makes them feel alive and powerful. The more turmoil they can create inside of them and around them by arousing others the more chemicals released into their blood stream and the higher they feel. Often the child picks a specific person to oppose because he or she is particularly vulnerable. If they cannot get others to buy into their behavior and help them escalate they internally escalate by focusing on negative and anxiety producing thoughts.

This behavior becomes addictive as the chemical release is so arousing, much like riding a roller coaster. Breaking the cycle of addiction to turmoil in a child is difficult but with patience and perseverence can be accomplished. Key is the adults must stay calm and must not contribute to the child's desire to escalate by escalating themselves. Yelling, hitting, sarcasm heighten the child's state of arousal. The opposite needs to occur. The louder the child, the softer the adult. The adult may excuse himself or use humor to defuse the situation. Listen and say once, "I would like to understand but can't help you when you are yelling." It is rarely effective to reason with an irrational child.

Another possibility is to use the "Broken Record" technique, "Go to your room. As soon as you are quiet for 10 minutes I will come and talk to you." Child yells or refuses. Parent says again, "Go to your room. As soon as you are quiet for 10 minutes I will come and talk to you." Child yells or refuses. Parent says again, "Go to your room. As soon as you are quiet for 10 minutes I will come and talk to you." Child yells or refuses. Parent says again.... Ad infinitum, until child capitulates or parent leaves.

<u>Ignoring Behavior</u>
The first, and least intrusive reactive parenting technique, is to simply ignore all behavior which can be ignored, such as sloppy dressing and careless schoolwork. Unkempt kids simply aren't invited on family outings and poor schoolwork has its own, built-in consequences. Children who have no sense of their own worth do not tend to take care of themselves in healthy ways. Poor hygiene is common. Other symptoms of attachment issues which can often be safely ignored at home are abnormal eating patterns, abnormal speech patterns and persistent nonsense questions and incessant chatter. Ignored behaviors often disappear on their own as the child and parent realize many behaviors are engaged in for shock value and without parental reaction they are not worth continuing.

There are much more dangerous and important behaviors to be addressed than these. These behaviors are not the problem, they are symptoms of the problem and attempting to control them will ultimately be fruitless and may be counterproductive. Removing them prematurely may only drive the child to find other ways to demonstrate their lack of attachment. The chances that replacement behaviors will be as benign as baby talk and silly questions are slim.

Many behaviors which are better ignored during the course of the day, however, may be addressed by the therapist and/or parent as a therapeutic (not a parenting) issue as they are usually indicative of a larger problem in the child's life.

Keep in mind there are three ways which the technique of ignoring behaviors can be used:
1. Behaviors are ignored by the parent.
2. Behaviors are ignored by the parent and referred to the therapist.
3. Behaviors are ignored for the moment, but consequenced later. Ignoring a behavior, if it is safe to, when it occurs allows the parent to give thought to an appropriate consequence and implement it when both the child and the parent are not emotionally involved.

Joining In

The opposite of ignoring is joining the child in the behavior. When the child tantrums throw yourself on the floor right next to them and scream and pound. It is helpful if every minute or so you look over at the child and ask them if you are doing it right. Or, when the child complains petulantly about what someone did, respond in kind and tell them in the same manner and similar choice of words about a time someone did the same thing to you. Or, come screaming out of your room that you haven't a thing to wear and you're going to flunk the spelling test. The possibilities are endless.

Distracting

Many children get locked into a negative response and brain pattern. They are not reacting negatively to the particular suggestion or request, they are reacting negatively because their brain's first response to everything is "No." Often the pattern can be interrupted by immediately dropping the subject, so as not to further entrench the resistance. Next, distract the child by going on to another subject or activity, read a book with the child or play a game. It is often useful to then come back and make the same suggestion or request later. After the child's brain has had a chance to subliminally process the original request and has come to the conclusion that a "yes" is in order, the child may be more agreeable. Dropping a subject and coming back later after the child has either been distracted or the friction has been defused is sometimes called "attack and retreat." It can be used repeatedly over the same issue. Children have honed this skill in order to wear down their parents' resistance. Parents can use the same technique to their own advantage.

Excuse Yourself

When it is apparent an impasse has been reached and only arguing is going to be the result it is perfectly appropriate for the parent to leave the scene. Saying, "Excuse me, I have to go to the bathroom," defuses the strife in mid-sentence and gives both parties an opportunity to avoid saying or doing they will later regret. Stay away as long as it takes for the child to calm down, as long as he is not being destructive or hurtful to others in the home.

Touch

The next least intrusive technique is a simple touch to remind children you are present and aware of their behavior. A hand rested lightly on the shoulder often is all that is necessary to help children become more thoughtful.

Bringing children in close with a gentle touch when they misbehave catches them off guard. Their defenses are up to ward off a physical or verbal blow. When a hug, accompanied by a sympathetic, "My, my. You must be feeling pretty bad inside in order for you to do that." comes instead, there is a lapse of their defenses which allows for a brief opportunity for parental acceptance to enter. This is a particularly effective response when children call their parents foul names or refer to them in vulgar terms. Language is very difficult to control and sometimes it is best to not get in an overt control battle over it. Disarming the child's need to lash out in this way is often more effective than confronting it. "I am sorry you feel that way as I love you very much" is one response. Another might be, "I wonder if someone has said such things to you and hurt you very badly. You must want to hurt me the way you were hurt. Well, I don't want to hurt you. Here's a hug. Hope you get over the need to say such things."

Attachment is created through myriad small, reassuring occasions such as these. Consequencing is essential, and is useful in keeping children from falling into disrespectful patterns, but it does not need to occur as a response to every negative behavior every time it happens. Don't underestimate the power of a smile accompanied by raised eyebrows, or a widely mouthed "I love you" to stop some unacceptable behaviors in their tracks.

Mom Time

"Mom time" is slightly more intrusive than touching as the child is brought in close after misbehavior and held or cuddled on the lap. Making a child feel loved and valued while giving him a chance to regroup and choose a different behavior is the goal. This can be for a few minutes or long enough to read him a couple of short storybooks. Afterwards the child can be given a consequence or sent off with a hug to try again.

"Mom time", when it is extended, becomes "line-of-vision- supervision". The child is kept within sight at all times. There are three rationales for what can be called the "umbilical cord":

1. The child can learn how to make good decisions concerning what to say, where to go to the bathroom, how to handle objects, etc. by observing another person making those decisions in a good way.

2. The child can be confronted with his behavior and told until he learns to make good decisions he needs to be close to someone who can make good decisions for him.

3. The child is to practice asking permission.

Children who have a negative world view have learned in order to survive they must be in control. Asking someone else for help or permission to do something is a relinquishment of their need to control and is psychologically very difficult. Being placed in a position where they need to ask permission to play with a toy, speak, go to the bathroom, or eat gives the child practice in asking permission and gives the parent opportunities to establish trust by saying "yes" to the requests as often as possible. The child learns he will not die if he allows someone else into his life.

Clearly, unless the supervisor can relax with it, line-of-vision-supervision can be very tiring for the supervisor, especially if it goes on for days or weeks, which is possible with unattached children.

Practice Sessions

Having "practice sessions" is another technique which is only minimally intrusive. Because the goal is to get the child to enjoy cooperating, the person conducting the session can be silly and pizazzy. Practice sessions are conducted at the parent's convenience, not necessarily when a behavior infraction occurs. A child who does something once for the parent is in a better position to comply twice. Having the child do something appealing or funny is an easier prelude to compliance than having them do something unwelcome.

"Please get a piece of candy from the dish for everyone" is an excellent way to initiate cooperation. "Run to the door and put your nose to the doorknob" can be incorporated into a game situation similar to 'Simon Says'.

After the child is cooperating he can be asked to do what he needs to practice, "Please go flush the toilet." "Please get in the car and buckle your seatbelt". When the child replies they didn't use the toilet, they are not going anywhere in the car, the parent says, "I know. This is just a practice session, so when you need to do it you know how." If the child won't do it, it is ignored for the moment. However, the next time he asks for something, the command is repeated. Dinnertime is often the next opportunity as the child almost invariably asks, "Please, pass the milk," and with a gentle smile the parent can say, "Please, go flush the toilet."

Sometimes a child will get mad and react in a negative way. If that occurs the parent needs to keep in mind if there is going to be anger over a child's behavior, it needs to be the child getting angry, not the parent. Often enough to make the technique worthwhile however, the child will smile and comply. If not, quietly stick to your intent without contributing to an escalation and then weigh whether or not it is something worth trying again with that particular child. The point of therapeutic parenting is not to do what doesn't work harder, but to do something different in hopes of finding something that will work.

A balance must be achieved between consistency, and unpredictability. Consistency is the child knowing there will be a consequence in response to a negative behavior. Unpredictability is not knowing what that consequence is going to be.

Practice sessions can also be conducted around negative behaviors which have become habitual. A parent can say delightedly to a child who has just spit, "I didn't know you liked to spit. This plant needs watering. Just start spitting right here until you are done." Though this has the potential to make an initial mess of the plant the child will soon tire of the "game" and will ask to quit. The parent then checks with the child, "Are you quite sure you are done spitting. I don't want you to stop until you have no more left in you." The goal is to get the child to state in a believable manner, "I am sure I am done spitting."

Anytime the parent engages in a technique such as this, however, it is critical to be aware of their tone of voice. These conversations must take place in a congenial manner. This is not the time for cruel wit or sarcasm.

A similar activity can be done around stealing and lying. Hiding in obvious places identifiable items for the child to steal and then having them practice "stealing" them is a way to get a covert activity out into the open where it can be dealt with. When the child is seen with the "stolen" item in his hand then he is gleefully chased through the house in a wild game which ends in wrestling and laughing and giggling on the part of both parent and child. When the child is successful in "stealing" the object when no one is watching, nothing occurs and the child gets no reinforcement.

Similarly a game can be devised where the goal is to tell the most outlandish lies. The better the lie the more guffawing and laughing. Lies told in the course of normal conversation get no reinforcement, negative or positive.

Having a child practice hearing the word "no" can be a fun activity while diffusing the need for control on the part of the child and helping the child realize being told "no" and not having total control over a situation does not threaten their survival.

"Let's play a new game. It is called the "No Game". I will tell you to do anything I want to and you need to tell me "No". Then you tell me to do anything you want to tell me to do and I am going to say "No." We'll take turns back and forth. I will start. Spell your name backwards. Stand on your head. Waddle like a duck. Say, 'I love you, mom'. (Each time the child responds with a negative.)"

The child then makes silly requests with the parent responding in the negative. The game then goes to asking for something with the parent beginning. "Please do the dishes." "May I have a hug." "Have you brushed your teeth." "Get yourself a piece of candy." No matter what the parent requests the rule dictates the child must answer "No". The child then asks the parent for something. "May I have more ice cream." "May I please go ride my bike".

"It is all right if I go do my homework now", etc. The parent must say "No" even if is something it would be wonderful for the child to do.

Sometimes it is the parent who needs to practice. Practicing dealing with those behaviors which they have found to be the most annoying can be very beneficial to removing the emotional content of the child's behavior. It is important for parents to know which of their children's behaviors have the most negative impact on them and so actively work to diffuse their reaction. This can be done in front of a mirror. Chewing with the mouth open while watching themselves in the mirror until the sight no longer bothers them is one way of getting to the point where a child cannot push a button with the parents over bad table manners. Screaming at the mirror, "You F---, A---, B---!" is a way of getting used to the sounds of foul language so the reaction when a child says it is impassive rather than emotional.

The Double Bind

Another technique that can be fun for parents is the "double bind". It is a paradoxical technique which allows for, and sometimes encourages, oppositional behavior in a way that keeps the parents in charge. This can be used in concert with several other techniques. The point is to tell the child to do what he is going to do anyway. If he does it, the parent is in control. If he doesn't he has made a right choice.

For example, "Go clean up your toys, but first, whine and cry." If the child righteously declares he can pick up his toys without whining and crying, the parent has won! If he whines and crys, the parent has still won!

"It's your turn to do the dishes, but don't worry, take your time, there's no rush. They'll still be there tomorrow, and the great thing is that there will probably be more then so you'll be able to help out even more than if you do them tonight."
"Feel free to not study for tomorrow's spelling test. Your dad and I are perfectly capable of loving a child who doesn't know how to spell."
"Keep practicing flipping the bird. If you are going to do something, do it until you are the absolute best at it!"

Try pizazz for good behavior plus a double-bind.
"Wow, did you see what you just did? You walked by Jim without punching him!!! I bet that was an accident. You meant to hit him and forgot. Walk by and try it again to see if I saw what I think I saw!"

One of the beauties of the double-bind is the parent gives the child permission to make a bad choice. When the child does make a bad choice, the parent is ready for it and does not get sucked into an angry response. It doesn't make sense to get angry at a child for doing what he has been told to do. Additionally, since many negative behaviors are done to enrage the parent, having the parent give permission often robs the child of the reason for doing it.

This is particularly useful when a child has had a very good day. Some children are so unaccustomed to good behavior they need to sabotage their success in order to get back to their more comfortable role of behaving badly. To diffuse the child's desire to fail it is helpful to say:

"It must feel pretty weird to not have people yelling at you all day. Don't push this being good thing too far. One day is enough. Tomorrow, relax, take it easy, try something sneaky just to keep in practice. See how often you can make people angry."

The child can then think, "I'll show Dad. He can't tell me what to do. I can too be good two days in a row." Or, he can think, "Dad's right. That was hard today. No point in setting everyone up to think I've changed when I really don't want to." Either way, everyone hopes for the best but is prepared for the worst, so whatever happens can be greeted with equanimity, rather than a sense of failure that one good day wasn't extended to two good days.

Repayment
Sometimes the best response to continued bad behavior is to declare, "You are draining my energy", or, "You're hassling me. Which chore do you want to do to fill me back up?" Then, list some of the things that need to be done and have the child choose one.

Having a child perform a necessary task creates a win-win, reciprocal situation because the parent is taken care of, so can continue loving the child without being blocked by anger, and the child feels good for doing something right, so feels entitled to the parent's love. However, a firm foundation in consequencing skills is a must. Assigning a chore and having no way to make sure it is done properly is signing a death warrant to winning control and subsequent trust.

A reactive technique used in response to lying and stealing is to impose a consequence on the basis of who is probably responsible. This gets parents out of the "proving it" game, which they almost are guaranteed to lose. Faced with either behavior a therapeutic parent is likely to impose a consequence on the probable violator and when the child protests he didn't do it say evenly, "What do you think I believe?" When the child says, usually petulantly, "You believe I did it!". The parent calmly says, "That's right", then imposes a consequence while assuring the child that if the wrong person has been held responsible then as soon as the parent is aware of their mistake they will repay the wronged child. This is a fairly safe technique with unattached children as they usually, despite their protestations, are responsible. Rarely have therapeutic parents had to repay a child wrongly consequenced!

An additional verbal message can be given if the child continues to protest his innocence. The parent can ask, "Have you ever stolen (or lied) and not gotten caught?" The answer is invariably in the affirmative. "Well, then this just makes up for all the times you did it and didn't get caught. In the end it will all work out evenly." Generally children are silenced by this reasoning as it makes perfectly good sense to them and they can see the truth in it.

Contracting

When it is clear what level of behavior a child can achieve parents can contract to ensure that behavior will predictably occur when it is most needed. One way to get a child to buy into good behavior is to arrange for the behavior in advance. Verbal or written agreement on a contract which outlines expected behavior and the consequence for poor behavior allows children to buy into the process of participating. It often becomes clear a child is not behaving appropriately because he does not want to be involved in the activity in the first place. Getting that out in the open before you go to the store, leave on a trip, attend a school activity helps you decide what to do next. Sometimes getting a babysitter, which the child pays for, or changing/postponing plans is in order. If plans cannot be changed a trade may be offered in exchange for good behavior. "You pull off spending one hour at the dentist's while I get my teeth cleaned and when we get home I will read to you."

Forcing children to be where they do not want to be, doing what they don't want to be doing, seeing people they don't want to see is a sure way to make sure no one has a good time. Being an effective parent requires taking care of yourself first and foremost. It's not good for children to sabotage parents' plans. Therefore, it's important that parents arrange events in such a way they are taken care of regardless of what the child chooses to do. What that means in extreme cases is the parent is deprived of participating in a desired activity. The natural consequence for the child is doing something for the parent to make it up. In therapeutic homes that translates into chores, big-time! Hopefully, when a child gets involved with a contract first, it will help him choose to participate and he will understand what behavior norms are acceptable.

Buying into that process in advance often is enough to ensure appropriate behavior, which is, after all, the goal!

Think-it over Spot

Another reactive technique involves having the child who has made a poor behavior choice go to a "think-it-over spot". This is a technique common to many classrooms. Instead of confronting a child with bad behavior, the child confronts himself. Whenever a child's behavior requires attention, he is told to sit in a designated spot (on a chair or the floor, back to the wall, facing the wall, whatever), until he can state, either out loud or in writing, what happened, how he felt, how he behaved, and how he will handle the same situation in the future.

Having the child simply sit, when behavior is problematic or non-compliant, with no directive on what to think, is another tool. Usually the child sits with his back to the wall, crossed legs, hands in his lap, back straight, head erect, eyes straight forward. That is good sitting. Rather than make a control battle out of it, however, it is not uncommon for a therapeutic parent to say, "You can either sit right for 10 minutes or sit sloppy for half an hour." That way the child can choose how long he wants to sit and how long he wants to think. Whichever he chooses, at the end of the allotted time, let him get up, give him a hug, get a reciprocal smile (or back to sitting), give him a "good luck" message and set him back to the task he was attempting before intervention.

Generally, if attachment is the goal of the therapeutic parenting, children who are not compliant are not sent to their room. Isolation may be exactly what the attachment disordered child prefers and it is counterproductive to reinforce it. Rather, sitting is implemented within sight, sound and touch of the parent who is available to intermittently intrude on the child with a hug or hair tousle and, "I sure am glad to know you are right where I can hug you whenever I want. I can hug you for half an hour when you sit sloppy. If you were sitting correctly you would be outside playing and then how would I hug you? Thanks for staying right where you are!"

There are other times when it is beneficial to have a child go to his room to think things over. In order for Rules 1, 2, & 3, regarding taking good care of yourself, to be adhered to, then occasions will arise when the child whose behavior is problematic will need to be separated from the rest of the family in order for the rest of the family to have a good time. The focus of the family must be on healthy relationships and all the fun that can be had when people are respectful, responsible and fun to be around.

When the energy of the family is directed to the child whose behavior is difficult than the child has an incentive to stay difficult in order to continue receiving the bulk of the parent's attention. Rather than hold the family hostage to bad behavior it is better to say, with great equanimity, "Hop off to your room so the rest of us can enjoy each other's company. We'll let you know when you can join us." This forces the child to see that if he wants to join in the fun he needs to set aside his anger and his angry behaviors. No child has gotten worse because he was forced to spend too much time in his room due to his own negative behaviors.

The same principle is operating when parents take a child whose behavior is predictably disruptive to a babysitter while the rest of the family participates in a fun activity. The point is not for the child at the sitter to have a bad time. He is welcome to have a great time, he just doesn't get to have a great time with the family.

Setting aside fun time for the family is not only an essential part of keeping healthy siblings healthy it also serves as a tool to draw angry children to the light.

Tickling and Touching

Since touch is a critical element of attachment work it becomes an integral part of any therapeutic parenting technique. Grabbing a child up into a big bear hug and lightly tickling him while encouraging him to get a task done gets him laughing and into a compliant frame of mind. The tickler laughingly says in accompaniment something like, "Who's the best bedmaker in the world?" or, "Who can empty the dishwasher all by himself?" until the child giggles, "Me!" A pre-teen child will then often skip off and do what is required with just a light tousling of the hair and quick, giggle inspiring tickles in the ribs. If this is not fun for both the parent and the child it must not be used.

Another time this is useful is for older children or when the child has behaved badly. Mock-wrestle and tickle the child as you laugh and say, "Do you think I'm the kind of mom who can only love good kids?" The goal is for the child to laughingly respond, "No." However, since unattached kids are extremely resistant, the first thing he will usually say is, "Yes." As long as you both are having fun the tickling can go another 60 seconds or until the child says, "No". Otherwise, in order to avoid allowing the child to take control of the interaction by persisting in a negative answer, stop the interaction with, "Sorry you believe that." End with a quick hug and, if the behavior needs a consequence, tell it lightly to the child.

Deposits and Withdrawals

One of the benefits of avoiding control battles is that parents build up a bank account filled with all the times they have said "yes" to their child. Then when the occasion arises and it is necessary to say "no" it can be put in the context of a larger picture in which permission is given more than it is denied. This only works when parents do, indeed, say "yes" more than they say "no".

One of our sons got some new pants for school and asked if he could wear them to soccer practice. Since they were his pants and we didn't want to hassle him over it we agreed. Once there he was asked to play goalie and he asked if he could wear them in the goal box, a very hard arena on clothes. They ripped so he came home and patched them on the outside, loving them just as much. He continued to wear them to practice. The patches ripped and he held them together with safety pins. He then asked if he could wear the pants to church. I gave it some thought and then denied the request. He became upset. I replied, "Am I usually pretty reasonable? Have I been letting you wear your new pants everywhere you wanted to wear them? Do I usually let you decide what you wear? Sorry, this time I'm deciding."

Before the subject of Reactive Techniques is left behind this thought needs to be boldly repeated. Make a poster and put it on your refrigerator!

Resisting Resistance Increases Resistance

What is required of the therapeutic parent is the ability to dance with the resistance, using the child's own momentum to propel them where you need them to be in order to take control in safe, nurturing, fun ways. A cowboy might call it "Heading 'em off at the pass." A soccer coach would tell the team, "Don't go to where the ball is. Go to where it will be next." The same principles apply to being an effective, thoughtful parent. The child will be expecting a frontal assault on his behavior. The parent accepts that that behavior has already occurred. Punitive measures to stop that event are already too late. What is required at that point is reactions on the part of the parent which will help create thoughtfulness in the child for the future while maintaining a present relationship.

Discipline vs. Punishment in Using Reactive Techniques

As parenting techniques become more intrusive, in response to the child's escalation of negative behavior, it is critical to remember that any technique can quickly become abusive. Professional therapeutic parents spend a great deal of time discussing when a technique constitutes thought-provoking discipline, used to bring a child's behavior into line, and when it becomes punishment, used to satisfy the anger needs of the parent.

One common understanding is that when the <u>parent</u> becomes angry, discipline is no longer therapeutic and should not be attempted until the parent is no longer emotionally over-involved. Another point of agreement - techniques which are not effective must be changed, not continually increased in intensity.

It must further be kept in mind that professional therapeutic parents have children in their homes for therapeutic care. The children are generally seen at least weekly by their therapist. An ideal session begins with the parent and therapist discussing the intervening days, what behaviors need immediate attention by the therapist, how the long-term goals were being reached, and, of great importance, what parenting techniques were used with what behaviors and with what results. These techniques are added to and modified until both the parent and therapist are comfortable with the direction the parent will take next.

Note that intrusive techniques are used only when both parent and therapist have a specific behavior modification goals in mind and agree that going forward with it are in the best interests of the child. Therapeutic foster parents do not operate in a vacuum and it is hoped that other parents will also be in consultation with an attachment therapist before using any intrusive therapeutic parenting technique.

Intrusive Reactive Parenting Techniques

With this in mind a few of the more intrusive techniques can be briefly explained. It is not expected a parent would use these techniques without consultation with an attachment therapist. Additional techniques are outlined by Richard Delaney and Frank Kunstal in Troubled Transplants, a book detailing unconventional strategies for helping disturbed foster and adopted children.

Increasing Blood Flow

A helpful way to create thoughtfulness and diffuse anger in children is to have them do something which requires a high degree of energy. Say to a child who is not completing a task well or has made a bad behavior choice, "In my experience a lot of kids find it easier to get their brain in gear when they have a higher blood flow. Do 25 jumping jacks and see if that is true for you as well." Getting compliance on one level often generalizes to another level. Since it is sometimes easier to get compliance with a jazzy activity rather than a chore, therapeutic parents may start with that. A small home trampoline is an ideal tool as it is difficult for a child to stay angry while jumping on it. After the child has done the push-ups, sit-ups, run around the block, waddled like a duck, whatever, let him return to his activity or chore and see if his behavior improves.

If it hasn't, there are two options: One is to assign it again, in a larger quantity, saying, "I'm sorry, I didn't know your brain was so hard to engage. This time do 35 jumping jacks and see if that helps you think more clearly." The other possibility is to switch tracks. "I see you aren't ready to even do sit-ups the way I know you can. Just sit by me until I'm ready to give you another opportunity to do what you need to do."

While the child sits it is all right for him to express his displeasure about the unfairness of life as long as he realizes that his negative verbalizations mark his sitting as poor sitting, not good sitting, so he must sit longer. When the child is able, with enthusiasm, to say, "I'm ready to do my sit-ups and then the dishes!", then they get the opportunity to do the simple activity and if done well then the more complex activity.

This can be repeated with some escalation, however, if it still doesn't move a child into thoughtfulness and compliance then it is back to the beginning premise, "You can do the wrong thing over and over or the right thing once."

Don't keep at a child with the same discipline technique if it isn't getting the desired results. Try something else, otherwise the child will end up digging himself deeper and deeper into a morass of consequences and he will not be able to get himself out. If a lose-lose situation is created where the consequence is escalating and the child is getting impossibly behind in compliance then the child may get discouraged and quit.

Correct Scolding

Shocking a child into compliance can occasionally be done with a one-minute scolding. This is definitely one of the more intrusive techniques. It also requires a good sense of timing on the part of the scolder. The goal is for the scolder to recreate in the child, in the space of one minute, the bonding cycle while modeling for the child that people can and do get angry, yet no one gets hurt. The child needs to be aroused, then comforted by the parent in order for the child to develop a sense of trust. A whole book, Who's the Boss?, by Gerald Nelson & Richard Lewak has been written on this technique.

Basically, the parent looks the child in the eye, places his hands on the child's shoulders and scolds the child severely, using rapid, fairly loud speech, until the child tears up or shows some sign of emotion.

The parent focuses in sharply on what the child did and why the parent is angry. The hard part is next. After the child tears up, the parent must have a marked drop in intensity and make a clear transition to being nurturing by bringing the child in close, telling him how much he is loved, and letting him know how much you want a better life for him. It is also important that the child sees how his behavior affects his life. The scolder needs to end with a hug, hopefully gain a reciprocal smile and a short question and answer session on what the child did wrong. The whole process needs to take between sixty and ninety seconds. If it takes too long than the child's thoughts wander, his brain disengages, even though he is physically present. This technique is most effective when used sparingly. One-minute scoldings administered weekly lose their effectiveness. An example:

One of the girls was using a can of spray paint in the laundry room, where the gas furnace is, and had closed the door to keep from getting caught. I walked in, caught her closely in my arms, and scolded her loudly with clipped sentences. "Stop that at once. That is a terribly dangerous thing to do and you knew it. Otherwise you would not have closed the door. That was very sneaky. You could have caught yourself on fire or created an explosion. You could have started the whole house on fire. I am very angry. (Having aroused her to tears I dropped in intensity and began to engage her face with eye contact.) Besides I love you. What would I have done if you had hurt yourself? You are my precious little girl. You scared me very badly. (Smiling, gentle tone, searching her face for a reciprocal smile.) Do you know what you did that was so dangerous? Will you promise not to do that again? Good girl. I love you."

Unblocking Rage

Oftentimes a child who is misbehaving or non-compliant is so blocked with rage that he cannot function. Unlocking that rage, and thereby freeing the child to do the right thing, can sometimes be accomplished by getting the child to yell what you believe he is feeling or thinking. Goals are two-fold: One is for the child to experience love and acceptance, even at the height of his rage. The second goal is to enable the child to release his rage at a time and place and in a way that it can be controlled.

If rage is not released in a safe way it can explode in a potentially dangerous manner. Not only is that not good for others in the child's environment but the child then must deal with all the damage and hurt he caused while he was enraged. Leaving a child in the situation where he continually has to deal with what he has done in the past leaves him with less energy to deal with present and future behavior. He becomes overwhelmed with defeat and a sense of hopelessness.

The first step in this technique is to face the child and gently place your hands on his shoulders. Very calmly suggest to him what you believe he is thinking and have him repeat it. "I won't do it your way"; "You can't make me vaccuum the floor"; "I hate doing the dishes"; "You're not my boss"; "You bitch." Or, a more accurate reflection of an unattached child's thoughts, "You fuckin' asshole bitch. I want to kill you." In a louder tone of voice tell him to say it louder. Everytime you tell him to repeat it, you do it in a louder tone and gradually work the child up to yelling. All this time bring your face closer and closer to his until you are almost nose to nose, until the child is yelling into the parent's face.

While the child is yelling it's important for the adult to empathetically focus on how hard the child is working to release his rage, rather than focusing on the anger directed at the parent. Otherwise the adult could get sucked into the child's rage.

When the child has reached a peak, usually within one and a half to two minutes, drop in intensity and bring him close in a hug. As in the one-minute scolding, closeness, hugs, gentle words and reciprocal smiles are essential to lock in the sense of relief and trust that tends to flood a child once he stops venting. This release is critical to a child's future ability to be trusting enough to be compliant. After a feeling of closeness is established, with a reciprocal smile and eye contact, have the child say, "I don't want to _____, and I'll do it anyway." Then, with one last hug, gently direct the child back to the unfinished, interrupted task.

Crisis Intervention

The most intrusive technique is reserved for when the child is physically lashing out in a rage and there are no alternatives to regain control. The point is to keep the child, other people or things, safe. The touch, therefore, is controlling to the point of being confining. Therapeutic parents at The Attachment Center at Evergreen are required to take a 12 hour course titled "Non-Violent Crisis Intervention", which teaches approved, safe holds. It is sponsored by the National Crisis Prevention Institute, 3315-K North 124th Street, Brookfield, Wisconsin, 53005. If there is a chance that a child's behavior will escalate to the point where a forced restraint is required, then the caretakers need to be trained to do that safely. This class is highly recommended.

Another nationally used system of physical restraints has been developed by Cornell University and is called the "Cornell Method". The training is extensive and information is available through Cornell University.

Both interventions emphasize de-escalation techniques and de-briefing methods with the child and others following any physical restraint.

Any discussion on intrusive techniques must end with the reminder they should be used only under the direction, supervision and training of an attachment therapist.

Consistency and Unpredictability

In most parenting patterns consistency in a wide range of parent-child interactions is important for them to be effective. In contrast, when parenting unattached children, the strength of the techniques often lies in their unpredictable use. Eye contact, touch, and the safety of the child need to be consistently present. However, with unattached children, it is necessary to "disturb the disturbed" and unpredictability becomes a crucial ingredient. When a child is acting the most unlovable, the parent needs to act the most unpredictable. It being predictable only that the parent is in charge and will handle all behavior in a good way.

A Sense of Self Worth is the Natural Result of Therapeutic Parenting

The building of self-esteem in a child has many components which therapeutic parenting techniques incorporate as fundamental to the success of forming a bonded parent-child relationship. They build self-esteem by:

1. setting up a home environment in which the child is safe, nurtured and respected.
2. taking care of the child in warm, stimulating ways through the provision of good food, generous time, hugs and touching, frequent smiles, and hopeful rituals.
3. modeling for the child that adults take good care of themselves, giving them the hope that when they grow up they will take good care of themselves as well.
4. modeling for the child that feelings are a wonderful part of being human and they can be expressed in safe ways.
5. modeling for the child that all people are worthy of respect and demonstrating intolerance for any words or behavior which are disrespectful to themselves or others.
6. teaching the child the importance of reciprocity in relationships.
7. holding the child accountable for unacceptable behaviors until they believe they, too, are capable of making excellent choices for themselves and others.
8. teaching the child to do chores so they acquire the ability to competently take care of themselves and others as adults.

In short, people feel good about themselves when they feel they are worth taking care of and they know they are competent to take care of themselves and others. Being given a responsibility and successfully following through on it can be euphoric. Children who are being given the responsibility to behave appropriately and taught the skills with which to do it feel good about themselves, others, and the world. They have a rightful place in the universe, they fit in and it feels very, very good.

In Closing

Take good care of yourself and understand there is an uncertainty principle operating in parenting. Just because you do it right does not mean it will work and just because you do it wrong does not mean it will fail. The determination for success or failure, whatever that means, is not in the hands of parents to decide. For some children, staying out of jail is success. For others, not abusing their spouse or children will be the measure of success.

Regardless, no act of love is ever wasted and all acts of love transform the lives of children, often in ways parents cannot discern or comprehend. Being the child of a parent who can love in therapeutic ways is the best thing that can happen to a reactive attachment disordered child. Few will affirm that for these special parents, often not even the child or society, but it is the truth nonetheless, and must be kept close to the heart when the pain of loving an unlovable child becomes too great to bear.

So....

Hug a child when he acts unlovable, not just when his behavior is good.

Pop a piece of candy in the child's mouth when he does well, and sometimes when he doesn't!

Ignore a behavior when it occurs and impose a consequence when the child doesn't expect it.

Laughingly/lightly help a child complete a task he has angrily/stubbornly stared at for hours.

Understand you may not be where you wanted to be, but you are where you are supposed to be.

These techniques, undergirded with a high regard for the child, a sense of humor and balance, a projection of strength even when it might be illusory, and a well trained support system, will go far to making an unattached child livable, and hopefully, ultimately, so lovable the parents are willing, eager and able to make a lifelong commitment.

Resources & Books Referred to in the Text

By Deborah Hage
For What It's Worth
Me and My Volcano

Parenting
Nighttime Parenting, William Sears
The Family Bed, Tine Thevenin
Developmental Play Therapy, Vi Brody
Messy Activities and More, Virginia Morin
Theraplay, Ann Jernberg and Phyllis Booth
When Love is Not Enough, Nancy Thomas
Holding Time, Martha Welch
The Mozart Effect, Don Campbell
Troubled Transplants, Frank Kunstal & Richard Delaney
Parenting with Love and Logic series, Foster Cline & Jim Fay

Brain Development
Change Your Brain, Change Your Life, Daniel Amen
Ghosts From the Nursery, Robin Karr-Morse & Meredith Wiley
Nature's Thumbprint - the Genetics of Personality, Peter & Alexander Neubauer

Diagnosis
Attachment, Trauma and Healing, Terry Levi and Michael Orlans
Cline/Helding Adopted and Foster Child Assessment, Foster Cline & Cathy Helding
Traits of a Healthy Family, Delores Curran

Alternative Forms of Healing
Aromatherapy Massage, Claire Maxwell-Hudson
Bodymind Workbook, Debbie Shapiro
The Complete Medicinal Herbal, Penelope Ody
Prescription for Nutritional Healing, James and Phyllis Balch

Attachment Symptoms and Differential Diagnosis

For many years those who work closely with behaviorally and emotionally problematic children with a history of foster care, institutionalization, abuse and /or neglect have discovered these children appear to have many behaviors in common. Research done by Dr. Liz Randolph points to a specific list of behaviors which have a strong correlation to Reactive Attachment Disorder.

The 30 item list is presented here as a <u>starting point</u> for those interested in exploring the presence or absence of RAD in a child they live or work with. In and of itself this list cannot be used to diagnose RAD without the scoring information, the taking of a detailed history and the assessment of previous testing and diagnosis. Background to the research, scoring of the symptoms list and conclusions which might be drawn from the response to the questionnaire are available through the Attachment Center at Evergreen.

Attachment Disorder Questionnaire-Revised

1. My child acts cute or charms others to get them to do what he/she wants.
2. My child has trouble making eye contact when adults want him/her to.
3. My child is overly friendly with strangers.
4. My child pushes me away or becomes stiff when I try to hug him/her, unless he/she wants something from me.
5. My child argues for long periods of time, often about ridiculous things.
6. My child has a tremendous need to have control over everything, becoming very upset if things don't go his/her way.
7. My child acts amazingly innocent, or pretends that things aren't that bad when he/she is caught doing something wrong.
8. My child does very dangerous things, ignoring how he/she may be hurt while doing them.
9. My child deliberately breaks or ruins things.
10. My child doesn't seem to feel age-appropriate guilt for his/her actions.
11. My child teases, hurts, or is cruel to other children.
12. My child seems unable to stop him/herself from doing things on impulse.
13. My child steals, or shows up with things that belong to others with unusual or suspicious reasons for how he/she got them.
14. My child demands things, instead of asking for them.
15. My child doesn't seem to learn from his/her mistakes and misbehavior (no matter what the consequence, the child continues the behavior).
16. My child tries to get sympathy from others by telling them that I abuse, don't

feed, or don't provide him/her with basic life necessities.

17. My child "shakes off" pain when he/she is hurt, refusing to let anyone comfort him/her.

18. My child likes to sneak things without permission, even though he/she could have had them if he/she had asked.

19. My child lies, often about obvious or ridiculous things, or when it would have been easier to tell the truth.

20. My child is very bossy with other children and adults.

21. My child hoards or sneaks food, or has other unusual eating habits (eats paper, raw flour, package mixes, baker's chocolate, etc.)

22. My child can't keep friends for more than a week.

23. My child throws temper tantrums that last for hours.

24. My child chatters non-stop, asks repeated questions about things that make no sense, mutters, or is hard to understand when he/she talks.

25. My child is accident-prone (gets hurt a lot), or complains a lot about every little ache and pain (needs constant band-aids).

26. My child teases, hurts, or is cruel to animals.

27. My child doesn't do as well in school as he/she could with even a little more effort.

28. My child has set fires, or is preoccupied with fire.

29. My child prefers to watch violent cartoons and/or TV shows or horror movies (regardless of whether or not you allow him/her to do this).

30. My child was abused/neglected during the first year of his/her life, or had several changes of his/her primary caretaker.

Using the Questionnaire

There is some value to having the questionnaire filled out by a variety of people who see and work closely with the child with the understanding that, typically, children with attachment issues behave better for people with whom there is only a superficial relationship. The closer the child is to the adult, the more the child will act out with that adult. Thus, when looking at the disparity between reports, the professional must not assume the adult who observes few behavioral issues is the "better" caregiver who utilizes "better" discipline techniques. It is far more likely the child does indeed behave better for a teacher or other adult because the child has less investment in the relationship. A child who has attachment issues will demonstrate far more severe symptoms with their parent, particularly their mother, than with anyone else. Even fathers will observe behaviors which are far more benign than the mother will experience as children with attachment issues do not tend to be as invested in the paternal relationship as the maternal relationship.

It is critically important that the professional, when looking at the variety of responses to the same Symptom Checklist, take each response as an indication of the range of behaviors which the child is capable of and not triangulate the responders by giving any message, subliminal or otherwise, the variety of responses is due in any way to the inability of the adult (particularly the mother) to be a loving, proficient, trusted caregiver. In other words, the variety of responses is reflective of the child's emotional lability. Grievous treatment errors could occur if it was assumed the variety of responses was reflective of the quality of care received at the hands of various caregivers.

The reality may rather be a negative correlation. That is, the better the behavior for a particular adult the more indifferent the attachment. The worse the behavior for a particular adult the more fearful the child is of forming an attachment and risking disappointment once again.

Some Thoughts on Differential Diagnosis

Many of the behaviors described on the Attachment Disorder Questionnaire would also correspond to the DSM-IV general diagnostic criteria for an adult Personality Disorder, with particular attention to Anti-Social Personality Disorder. There are also similarities to DSM-IV diagnostic criteria for Conduct Disorder and Oppositional Defiant Disorder. Additionally, children who have Attachment Disorder have many of the same symptoms as children with other childhood disorders such as ADD, Mood Disorder or Fetal Alcohol Syndrome. That is because when the ability to attach and love is not present, it effects many other aspects of living, behaving and responding. As attachment takes place early in life, the history of the child with ADD, FAS and mood disorder almost always shows early breaks in the mother child relationship so an overlap of diagnosis is possible. Thus, taking a complete history of the first two years of life is critical to an accurate diagnosis.

Much care must be given to accurate diagnosis as appropriate treatment is dependent on knowing exactly what is being treated. Medications and other interventions have the potential for optimum effectiveness when the therapeutic goal is clearly defined and other possible diagnosis are considered before being ruled out. To give all children Ritalin for hyperactive and unfocused behavior when the behaviors are driven by RAD and not ADHD is like giving an aspirin for diabetes.

Dr. John Alston has developed a useful differential diagnosis tool which helps parents and professionals decide whether the child is affected primarily by ADD, Bipolar I Disorder or Reactive Attachment Disorder. His chart follows.

Characteristics of Attention Deficit Disorder, Bipolar I Disorder and Reactive Attachment Disorder

Symptoms	**Attention Deficit Disorder, with or without hyperactivity**
Age of Onset	Infancy - toddler, 6, 13
Family History	ADHD, academic difficulties (based on task completion), alcohol and substance abuse
Lifetime Prevalence	Approximately 3-6% of general population
Etiology	Genetic, neurochemical, fetal development, brain traumas, nutritional deficiencies, exacerbated by stress
Duration	Chronic and unremittingly continuous, tending toward improvement
Attention Span	Short, leading to lack of productivity and task performance and completion
Impulsivity	Secondary to inattention or obliviousness, regret and remorse
Hyperactivity	50% are hyperactive. Disorganized, fidgety, jittery
Self-esteem	Low, rooted in ongoing performance difficulties
Mood	Usually friendly in a genuine manner. Some irritability

John F. Alston, M. D.
30752 Southview Drive, Ste. 100, Evergreen, CO 80437
Phone: (303) 670-0926   FAX: (303) 670-1191

<table>
<tr><td>

Bipolar I Disorder,
Mixed Type, (Rapid Cycling)

2-3, 6, 13-25

Any mood disorder (depression or bipolar), academic difficulties, based on motivation problems or opposition or defiance, alcohol and substance abuse, adoption, ADHD

1-3% of general population

Genetic, exacerbated by stress and hormones

May or may not show clear emotional and behavioral episodes and cyclicity; worsens over years with increased severity of symptoms

Entirely dependent on interest and motivation, distractibility common

"Driven," "Irresistible," grandiosity, thrill-seeking, counterphobia, little regret or remorse. Pressured speech.

Wide ranges, with hyperactivity common in children

Low because of inherent unpredictability of mood. Grandiose or expansive mood could mask low esteem

Unpredictable, oversensitive, expansive, hard to please or satisfy, grandiose, irritable

</td><td>

Reactive Attachment Disorder,
Disinhibited Type

Birth to 3

Abuse and neglect, severe emotional and behavioral disorders, alcohol and substance abuse, abuse and neglect in parent's own early life

Uncommon to common

Psychophysiologic secondary to neglect, abuse, mistreatment, abandonment

Dependent on life circumstances, age of relinquishment, including innate treatment and temperament. Worsens over years without treatment, develops antisocial character disorders

Hyperarousal influences hypervigilance, distractibility and shortened periods of focus. Shortens with stress.

Poor cause and effect. No remorse. Can range from overreactive to highly controlled, self protective.

Common

Low, rooted in abandonment, feel worthless and unlovable, masked by anger or indifference

Superficially charming, phony, distrusting, emotionally distance, nonintimate

</td></tr>
</table>

Control Issues	Desire to seek approval - get into trouble by inability to complete tasks.
Opposition/Defiance	Demonstrate argumentativeness but will relent with show of authority, redirectable. Short attention span allows them to "let go" easily
Blaming	Self-protective mechanism to avoid immediate adverse consequences
Lying	Avoid immediate adverse consequences
Anger, Irritability, Temper and Rage	Situational, in response to over-stimulation, poor frustration tolerance and need for immediate gratification. Rage reaction is usually short-lived
Entitlement (Deserving of Special Benefits)	Overwhelming need for immediate gratification (Not a prominent symptom)
Conscience Development	Capable of demonstrating remorse when things calm down. Close to developmental age
Sensitivity	Oblivious to detailed circumstances they are in and inappropriateness shows as result. Do get "big picture"
Perception	Flooded by sensory over stimulation, distractible, hyperactive or shut down
Peer Relationships	Makes friends easily but not able to keep them, immature
Sleep Patterns	Occasional trouble getting to sleep. Over-stimulated and physically wound up, once asleep "sleep like a rock." Fidget even in sleep. Nightmares uncommon.
Sexuality	Emotionally immature and sexually naive

Intermittently desire to please but tend to push limits and relish power struggles. Expert hasslers, persuasive

Controlled and controlling, only for self-gain, underhanded, sneaky and covert

Usually overtly and predominantly defiant, at times passive aggressive, often not relenting to authority. Tend to insist on getting own way

Conning and cunning. Covertly defiant, passive aggressive

Grandiosity contributes to disbelief/denial they caused something to go wrong

Rejecting of responsibility. Victim position

Enjoys "Getting away with it"

"Crazy lying," stuck in self-centered "primary process" distortions used to gain control

Secondary to limit-setting or attempts to control their excessive behavior, rage can last for extended periods of time, at other times may be explosive and over quickly. Overt, aggressive and assaultive

Chronic, revenge "get even" oriented. Eternal "victim" position, with rationalization for destructive retaliation. Hurtful to innocent others and pets

Expansive and grandiose mood creates belief they deserve special treatment

Compensation for abandonment and deprivation (Not a prominent symptom)

Limited conscience development, dependent on mood and parenting ability

Very "street smart," good survival skills, con artist, calculating, devious

Acutely aware of circumstances and are "hot reactors"

Hypervigilant, compensating for past helplessness. Resistant and insensitive, rarely ill. Limited emotional repertoire

Self-absorbed, preoccupied with internal need fulfillment, appears narcississtic. Dissociation possible. Inappropriare affect.

Self-centered primary process primitive distortions. Dissociation possible

Can be charismatic or depressed, depending on mood - conflicts are the rule due to controlling nature

Very poor. Secondary to lack of intimacy a nd control issues. Target others to get angry. No long term friends

Inability to relax, wind down because of racing thoughts, nightmares common

Hypervigilance creates light sleepers. Tends to need little sleep, arises early in a.m.

Sexual hyperawareness, pseudo-maturity, high interest and activity level

Uses sex as means of power, control or infliction of pain, sadistic

Motivation	Less resourceful, more adult dependent. OK starters, poor finishers
Learning Characteristics	Most common auditory perceptual difficulties and fine motor uncoordination. "Right brained"
Anxiety	Uncommon, unless performance related
Alcohol and Substance Abuse	Strong tendencies, out of coping mechanisms for low self-esteem
Firesetting	Play with matches out of curiosity
Parenting Techniques	Support, encouragement, redirection
Optimal Environment	Low stimulation and stress, support and structure. Identify learning disability components or psychological factors
Psychopharmacology	Medications helpful include Ritalin, Dexedrine, Cylert, Dexedrine, Adderall, Wellbutrin. Clonidine and Guanfacine may be useful as additive medications
Prognosis	Good to excellent with appropriate medical treatment, ancillary therapies and educational accommodations

Grandiose, believe they are resourceful, gifted, creative. Self-directed, highly variable energy and enthusiasm	Consistently poor initiative, limited industriousness, intentional inefficiency. Motivation for short term only
Non-sequential, non-linear learners, verbally articulate, used in shrewd and manipulative ways	Brain maturational delays secondary to maternal drug-alcohol effects, early life abuse/neglect can create diverse learning problems
Emotionally wired. High potentials for anxiety, fears and phobias. Somatic symptoms common, needle phobic. Dissociation	Appear invulnerable. Poor recognition, awareness or admission of fears. Dissociation
Very strong tendencies in attempt to enhance or reduce hypomanic/dysphoric moods	Sporadic/uncommon: not likely to be willing to lose that much control. Need more knowledge of correlation
Intrigued with matches/firesetting and can have malicious intent	Revenge motivated, malicious, danger seeking, secondary to despair
Nothing works long term until correctly diagnosed and medically treated	Understanding child's vulnerabilities and resistance aids in being workable
Clear and assertive, balance of limits, encouragement, negotiation. Helpful if all members of treatment team work together	Challenging balance of security, stability, clarity and unambiguity of expectations, nurturance and encouragement and love
Medications helpful to stabilize mood include: Lithium, Valproate, Verapamil, Carbamazepine, and Gabapentin. Medications helpful for rage and opposition reactions include: Olanzapine, Risperidone, Quetiapine and Ziprasidone. Antidepressants in small doses help mood and motivational enhancement	Antidepressants, Clonidine, Guanfacine may help decrease hypervigilance. Medications to not help characterological traits.
Fair to good with times of regression even with appropriate treatment	Highly variable, dependent upon recognition of comorbid mood disorders, degree of abuse/neglect, age of relinquishment, innate temperament and treatment

Parenting With Pizazz
A lecture series offered by Deborah Hage, MSW

Leadership Secrets of Atilla the Hun - See yourself as the leader in your family, take control in high morale building ways.
* Setting family tone
* Importance of reciprocity in relationships
* Importance of family rituals and traditions
* Dealing with control hassles

Parenting with Pizazz - Learn the art of consequencing. Have fun getting your child to cooperate.
* Making a child feel loved
* Deciding whose problem is whose
* Differences between consequencing and punishment
* The art of consequencing

Options to Anger - Ever feel like exploding? Concrete suggestions on channeling that energy into positive directions.
* Role of parental anger
* Placing responsibility for child's behavior on the child
* Specific techniques and interventions

Bonding and Attachment - What it is - What attached and stressed attached kids look like and how they behave. Signs and symptoms of attachment issues.
* Importance of attachment, bonding cycle and breaks in the bond
* Factors in personality development
* 1st and 2nd year attachment milestones
* Signs of problematic attachment

Parenting Techniques that Reinforce Attachment - Hands on techniques every parent can use to enhance their child's bond to them.
* Parent-child activities which promote attachment
* Encouraging the appropriate expression of feelings
* Re-doing early developmental stages in a good way
* Demonstrating affection with a resistant child

Teenagers! - With the right stuff these years can be filled with joy and laughter. How do you make parent and teen relationships work and what are the parental options when there is too little joy?
* Adolescent issues & corresponding parenting issues
* Keeping a behaviorally problematic teen at home
* How to decide when out-of-home placement is appropriate
* Letting go, emancipation, birth family issues

Fetal Alcohol Syndrome - FAS presents unique problems to families and others who would help victims. Understanding the developmental issues as the children move through childhood into adolescence and adulthood will enable professionals in schools, human services, medicine, law enforcement and vocational rehabilitation to be more effective.
* Cause and prevalence, Diversity of effects - benign to severe
* Ages & stages - how they differ from "normal" childhood development
* Developmental needs in infancy, toddlerhood, school, adolescence, and adulthood
* Hope for the future

About the Author

Deborah Hage remains happily married after 30 years and 14 children to Paul Hage. During the last 26 years of being parents they have given birth to two children, adopted seven children and have been therapeutic foster parents to five other children. Most of the children have been physically, emotionally, behaviorally and/or intellectually challenged. They have dealt extensively with Fetal Alcohol Syndrome, educational and legal issues. At one point in time 10 of the children were teenagers at once! Their oldest children are now in the throes of emancipation, with several seeking out and finding birth parents, one becoming a parent and others finding the surest way to leave home is to go to jail.

In her **"Parenting With Pizazz"** lectures Deborah shares how they have stayed sane through the trials and triumphs of parenting their children, most of whom entered their lives with emotional scars due to abuse and neglect. She lectures nationwide and in Canada on bonding and attachment as well as techniques which, when added to normal parenting styles, have a positive effect on children who are behaviorally problematic. Her presentations include information on how to make it more fun to be a parent and children more fun to be around, as well as when to hang on and when to let go. Interventions which are appropriate at home for children who are a danger to themselves, their family and/or their community are addressed.

Deborah has contributed chapters and articles on therapeutic parenting to several books and publications and has a master's degree in Social Work. She is in private practice and is available for consultation and intensive child and family therapy interventions.

For more information regarding two week intensive therapy, lecture dates and fees contact:
Deborah Hage, MSW
Parenting With Pizazz
P.O.Box 42
Silverthorne, CO 80498

970-262-2998 (FAX & Answering Machine)
e-mail Deborah@deborahhage.com
website http://www.deborahhage.com

Order Form

Name _____

Address _____City _____State_____

Zip _____Telephone _____

____copies of the book **When Love is Not Enough** at $15 _____
    A guide to parenting children with Reactive Attachment Disorder

____copies of the book **Dandelion on My Pillow, Butcher Knife Beneath** $19.95_____
    True story of an amazing family that lived with and loved kids who killed!

____copies of the 60 minute video **Circle of Support** at $15 _____
    Explains RAD & gives great support ideas for friends and family

____copies of **Healing Trust: Rebuilding the Broken Bond** audio at $18.95_____
    Two humorous cassettes or CDs, 3 hours, explains RAD & many "how to's"

____copies of the 3 1/2 hr DVD set **Captive in the Classroom** at $30 _____
    Presents powerful techniques & tools to ID and redirect disturbed students

____copies of the 2 1/2 hr video set **Give Me A Break** at $29.95_____
    Information baby sitters need to be highly effective to provide relief.

____copies of the 60 min. video **Building Brilliant Brains** at $15 _____
    Understanding and healing traumatized childrens' brains. Shows PROOF!

____copies of **Ask Nancy** –DVD - answers to 30 most frequently $15 _____
    asked questions from parents, teachers, and professionals

____copies of **Mastering Steps to Reach Children with RAD** / at $79.95_____
    When Love Is Not Enough - Changing parenting from Mystery to Mastery

____copies of **It's Not Just Horsing Around with Defiant Kids!** at $89.95_____
    Three DVD's & 175 pg manual w/ full lesson plan for horseback interventions

____copies of the Audio cassette set **Biology of Behavior** at $20.95_____
    Shares effective nutrition treatment ideas for attention and aggression.

____copies of **99 Ways to Drive Your Child Sane** booklet by St. Clair at $10 _____
    Wild ideas to add hysterical humor to a home with a disturbed child

____copies of **Therapeutic Parenting** book by Deb Hage MSW at $9 _____
    Wisdom from experienced Mom and great Attachment Therapist

____copies of **Me and My Volcano** workbook at $5 _____
    Anger management workbook by Deborah Hage, MSW

____copies of **So You Want To Be A Princess?** book at $4 _____
    Clever insightful children's book for girls by Deborah Hage, MSW

____copies of **So You Want To Be A Prince?** book at $4 _____
    Clever insightful children's book for boys by Deborah Hage, MSW

____copies of **Neurofeedback & QEEG Questions & Answers** at $4 _____
    Audio CD by Attachment Therapist, Larry Van Bloem, LCSW

____copies of **Broken Hearts; Wounded Minds** book by Liz Randolph PhD $34.95_____
    . 250 pgs of past and current research in a power packed manual

____copies of **Children Who Shock and Surprise** booklet $15 _____
    by Liz Randolph, MSN, PhD, leading researcher, parenting & treatment ideas.

Order totals	Add
Up to - $30	$ 4
$31 - $45	$ 7
$46 - $90	$ 10
$91 - $150	$14
$151 - $300	$18
$301 - $600	$22

Payable to: Families by Design   sub total _____
PO Box 2812
Glenwood Springs, CO   S & H _____
81602
970-984-2222   Total enclosed _____